Jackie Robinson

BREAKING THE COLOR
LINE IN BASEBALL

By Matt J. Simmons

Crabtree Publishing Company
www.crabtreebooks.com

Crabtree Publishing Company
www.crabtreebooks.com

Author: Matt J. Simmons
Publishing plan research and development:
 Reagan Miller
Project coordinator: Mark Sachner,
 Water Buffalo Books
Editors: Mark Sachner, Lynn Peppas
Proofreader: Shannon Welbourn
Indexer: Gini Holland
Editorial director: Kathy Middleton
Photo researcher: Water Buffalo Books
Designer: Westgraphix/Tammy West
Production coordinator and prepress
 technician: Margaret Amy Salter
Print coordinator: Katherine Berti

Written, developed, and produced by
Water Buffalo Books

Photographs and reproductions:
Alamy: © Everett Collection Inc: pp. 30, 51 (bottom),
67. **Associated Press:** cover (background); Harry
Harris: cover (background). **Corbis:** © Bettmann/
CORBIS: pp. 7, 59, 69 (bottom), 71, 78, 79, 98, 99; © RAY
STUBBLEBINE/Reuters/Corbis: p. 103. **Getty Images:**
pp. 13, 29, 31, 45, 54, 64, 73; NY Daily News via Getty
Images: p. 65. **Library and Archives Canada:** Ronny
Jaques: pp. 33, 66. **Library of Congress:** pp. 1, 4, 6, 15,
16, 17, 37, 46, 48–49, 53, 56, 70, 75, 80, 83, 85, 87, 97.
National Archives and Records Administration:
pp. 36, 39, 41, 42, 81, 89 (bottom), 90, 92 (both). **Public
domain:** pp. 9, 10, 21, 22, 60 (top), 76, 86, 94, 101.
Shutterstock: Callahan: p. 18; Philip Pilosian: p.
25; Krylova Ksenia: p. 26; ducu59us: p. 60 (bottom);
catwalker: p. 77; Jaguar PS: p. 102. **Wikipedia Creative
Commons:** jtesla16: pp. 5, 13 (top), 29 (top), 51 (top), 69
(top), 89 (top); Musée McCord Museum: p. 62.

Cover: At a time when much of the United States was
still racially segregated, Jackie Robinson smashed the
color barrier to become the first African American to play
baseball in the modern major leagues. He is shown
here in a team photo with fellow members of the Brooklyn
Dodgers.

Publisher's note:
All quotations in this book come from original sources and
contain the spelling and grammatical inconsistencies of
the original text. Some of the quotations may also contain
terms that are no longer in use and may be considered
inappropriate or offensive. The use of such terms is for
the sake of preserving the historical and literary accuracy
of the sources and should not be seen as encouraging or
endorsing the use of such terms today.

Library and Archives Canada Cataloguing in Publication

Simmons, Matt J., 1980-, author
    Jackie Robinson : breaking the color line in baseball / Matt
Simmons.

(Crabtree groundbreaker biographies)
Includes index.
Issued in print and electronic formats.
ISBN 978-0-7787-1242-8 (bound).--ISBN 978-0-7787-1244-2
(pbk.).--ISBN 978-1-4271-7482-6 (pdf).--ISBN 978-1-4271-1571-3
(html)

    1. Robinson, Jackie, 1919-1972--Juvenile literature. 2.
Baseball players--United States--Biography--Juvenile literature.
3. African American baseball players--Biography--Juvenile
literature. I. Title. II. Series: Crabtree groundbreaker biographies

GV865.R4S54 2014   j796.357092   C2014-903222-6
                                              C2014-903223-4

Library of Congress Cataloging-in-Publication Data

Simmons, Matt J.
 Jackie Robinson : breaking the color line in baseball / Matt J.
Simmons.
        pages cm. -- (Crabtree groundbreaker biographies)
    Includes index.
    ISBN 978-0-7787-1242-8 (reinforced library binding : alk. paper)
-- ISBN 978-0-7787-1244-2 (pbk. : alk. paper) -- ISBN 978-1-4271-
7482-6 (electronic pdf : alk. paper) -- ISBN 978-1-4271-1571-3
(electronic html : alk. paper)
 1. Robinson, Jackie, 1919-1972--Juvenile literature. 2. Baseball
players--United States--Biography--Juvenile literature. 3. African
American baseball players--Biography--Juvenile literature. I. Title.

 GV865.R6S55 2014
 796.357092--dc23
 [B]
                              2014017795

Crabtree Publishing Company
www.crabtreebooks.com   1-800-387-7650   Printed in Canada/052014/MA20140505

**Published
in Canada**
Crabtree Publishing
616 Welland Ave.
St. Catharines, Ontario
L2M 5V6

**Published in
the United States**
Crabtree Publishing
PMB 59051
350 Fifth Ave., 59th Floor
New York, NY 10118

**Published in the
United Kingdom**
Crabtree Publishing
Maritime House
Basin Road North, Hove
BN41 1WR

**Published
in Australia**
Crabtree Publishing
3 Charles Street
Coburg North
VIC, 3058

Contents

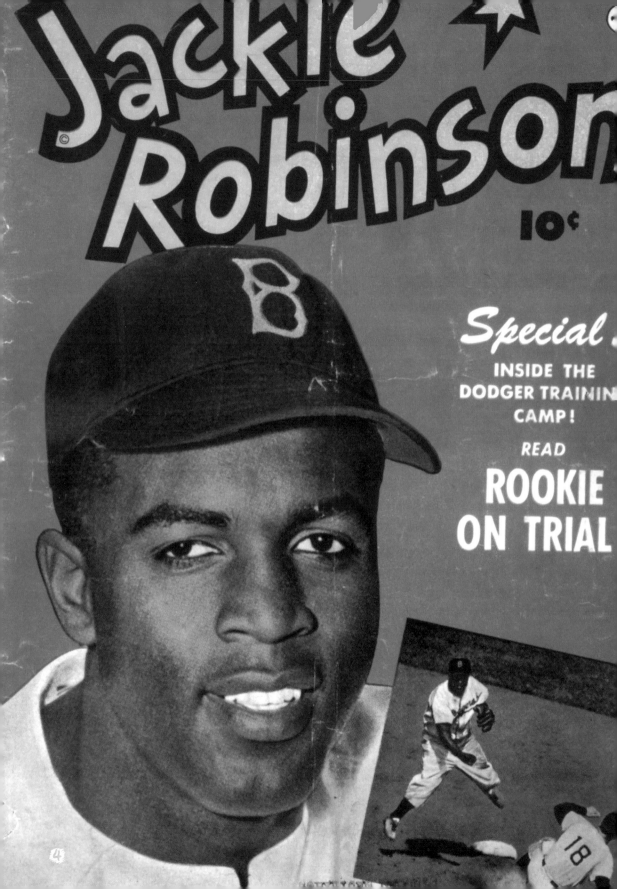

Chapter 1
The Color of Baseball

April 18, 1946, is a sunny spring day at Roosevelt Stadium in Jersey City, New Jersey. It's the first game of the season for two baseball teams in the International League. The Montreal Royals, the top minor-league team linked with the major-league Brooklyn Dodgers, are facing off against the Jersey City Giants, the top affiliate of the rival New York Giants. It's a perfect day for baseball, and the ballpark, built to hold 23,000 fans, is bursting at the seams with 52,000 people crammed into the stands. These fans aren't here just because it's a good day for a ball game. They are also here to witness a pivotal moment in history. It's the first modern-day appearance by an African-American baseball player in the minor leagues. That player's name is Jackie Robinson.

A Game to Remember

With his stomach churning, Jackie stepped up to the plate at just after three in the afternoon. He was a tall, broad-shouldered man, athletic and full of energy. The fans edged forward on

This sculpture of Jackie Robinson's number 42 at Citi Field, the home of the New York Mets, serves as a memorial to the man and his legacy. The team on which Jackie played his entire major league career, the Brooklyn Dodgers, left New York for Los Angeles in 1958.

Opposite: This Jackie Robinson *comic book (issue #5, 1951) attests to the star appeal of the Brooklyn Dodgers' second baseman. The inset shows Jackie leaping to avoid a sliding runner as he completes a double play. He led the National League in completed double plays during the 1950 and 1951 seasons.*

Jersey City mayor Frank Hague throws out the first pitch on Opening Day of the 1946 season at Roosevelt Stadium. That day, fans packed the ballpark by more than twice its capacity of 23,000. They were there to witness a moment in history—the breaking of what was known as baseball's "color line" by a young African-American player named Jackie Robinson.

their seats, a few cheering as the nervous player walked onto the field, his light gray uniform pale against the darkness of his skin. Many spectators were African Americans who had walked across the Hudson River to Jersey from the Harlem neighborhood of New York City to witness this moment. Jackie's new wife, Rachel, paced in the stands, so nervous for her husband that she couldn't sit still. New York and New Jersey reporters from both black and white papers watched expectantly from the press box.

After working the pitch count to three balls and two strikes, Jackie finally hit a grounder and was easily thrown out at first. It wasn't the breakthrough everyone was hoping for, least of all Jackie himself. But the next time he came to bat, he showed the world one of the reasons he had been chosen to be the first African-American playing baseball in the modern-era big leagues. Two of his teammates were on base, and Jackie's bat met the pitch with such force that the ball smoothly sailed all the way back into the left-field stands—home run. With a huge grin on his face, he trotted around the bases.

As Jackie rounded third, the Royals' manager, who had earlier begged the Dodgers not to assign Jackie to his team, gave him a pat on the back. Even the home crowd, which had no love for the visiting Royals, cheered him, and the runners who had scored ahead of him congratulated him as all three trotted back to

the dugout. It was the moment Jackie needed to shake off his nerves, and he went on to play a great game.

A fast runner despite his size, he stole second base twice. While on third, he repeatedly danced off the bag, ready to steal home. The pitcher threw to third twice trying to catch him off the bag, but Jackie dove back safely both times. The catcher even tried to throw him out once, but Jackie was too quick. When he danced off the base again, the pitcher was so flustered that he balked—stopping his pitch halfway—and Jackie was awarded home, scoring a run for the Royals. The fans, black and white alike, cheered him. It was the kind of baseball that was exciting to watch, and they loved what they saw.

For Jackie, the day was a success in every way. The Royals won handily, 14–1. He had made his official debut as the first African-American ballplayer signed to a professional-

Jackie Robinson crosses home plate after belting a three-run homer on Opening Day of the Montreal Royals' 1946 season. Teammate George Shuba (number 13) greet him at the plate.

level team in a sport that had been racially segregated almost since its beginnings in the 1800s. And in his first game, he'd shown everyone that he was a great ballplayer. He was nervous, of course, but his love of baseball gave him the strength to forget the world was watching and focus on the game. "Above anything else, I hate to lose," he said.

Baseball Breakthrough

After the game, thousands of fans surrounded Jackie as he tried to leave the stadium. Everyone wanted to congratulate the rookie. His skills at the sport had captured the imagination of every fan at the game: white, black, young, and old. Most newspaper stories about Jackie only partly talked about his abilities as a baseball player. Many of the headlines focused on the story about a man who had just made history.

In the 1940s, baseball was still strictly segregated by color. There was an unwritten ban, known informally as the "color line," against black baseball players. All professional-level players were white. There were a few Hispanic and other light-skinned minority players before Jackie's debut, but American players of African descent weren't allowed into the game.

Opposite: Moses "Fleet" Walker was one of a very few African-American players who were on rosters of otherwise all-white teams before baseball's color line became deeply drawn in the 1880s. Here he is shown, third from the right in the front row, on the University of Michigan team in 1882.

"We all sensed that history was in the making, that the long ban against Negro players was about to come crashing down, setting up reverberations that would echo across a continent and perhaps around the world."

Jackie Robinson

BASEBALL'S COLOR LINE

As it was with many facets of American life, racial segregation was a part of baseball from its beginnings in the 1800s until the middle of the 20th century.

In baseball's early days, some teams had white and black players. African-American teams also developed and played against white teams. But when the game became more organized and leagues began to form, the color line came into effect. While it wasn't an official rule, at least not in most leagues, it was an informal understanding that blacks and whites should not mix on the field of play.

In 1867, a black team from Philadelphia called the Pythian Base Ball Club applied for membership in the National Association of Base Ball Players (NABBP). That same year, the NABBP, which was the first organization governing American baseball, voted to exclude any team with players of African descent. The NABBP's decision became baseball's first official color line.

In the late 1800s, baseball continued to grow in popularity and size. Professional players earned a decent salary. Leagues became more organized. Unlike the NABBP, most leagues left the practice of segregation informal, and for a few years black players appeared on the rosters of otherwise all-white teams in the minor leagues, including the International League.

Then, in the 1880s, Cap Anson, a popular player from the time, began to make public demands that black players be removed from organized leagues. He even famously refused to play in any game where the opposing team had a black player on its roster. In 1887, the International League officially banned any club from adding African-American players to its roster. By 1890, that league was entirely white, and would remain so until 1946, when Jackie Robinson joined the Montreal Royals.

In the 1890s, the major leagues unofficially decided to ban blacks from their rosters. By the early 1900s, baseball's color line was completely drawn, and the professional leagues were entirely segregated.

Segregation based on the color of a person's skin was deeply entrenched in most aspects of American culture, and sports were no exception. There was such prejudice at the time that many Americans thought of black players—and black people in general—as less capable, even subhuman. All of the major and minor leagues were white-only. But the population of African-Americans throughout the United States was increasing steadily, and that population included many baseball players and fans.

Before Jackie stepped onto the field wearing a Montreal Royals jersey, the only place that an African-American could play ball professionally was in one of the all-black Negro Leagues.

After Jackie's first International League game that day, it was clear to the world that times were changing.

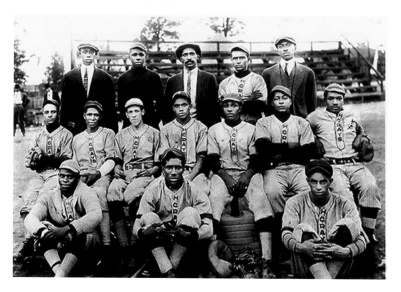

A team photo of the Homestead Grays, taken in 1913. Based in and around Pittsburgh and, later, Washington, D.C., the Grays were one of the most successful franchises in the history of the Negro Leagues. They remained in continuous operation for 38 seasons.

THE NEGRO LEAGUES

As racial segregation in baseball developed, grew, and became entrenched in the form of baseball's color line, America's black population also continued to grow. Official leagues informally or formally excluded African Americans, but that didn't mean black players stopped playing baseball. Instead, they organized their own leagues. The first few of these were so disorganized and poor that they were almost entirely unsuccessful. One of the earliest was the National Colored Base Ball League. It was formed in 1887 and lasted only two weeks. Several similar attempts floundered and failed, but in 1920, the Negro National League was successful in completing a full season of play. That year, it consisted of eight teams, and by its end in 1931 it had 24.

Other leagues formed in the 1920s and 1930s, including the Negro American League, which lasted until around 1960. Compared to the white leagues of the time, the Negro Leagues were poorly funded. While attendance was often high—the growing African-American population enjoyed baseball as much as their white counterparts—the stadiums were typically rundown and the fields in poor condition. Black players earned far less than white players in either the big-league National and American Leagues or even in such top minor leagues as the International League.

Following the signing of Jackie Robinson by the Brooklyn Dodgers, talented black ballplayers began filling major-league ranks in significant numbers. At the end of the 1948 season, the Negro National League folded, leaving only the Negro American League as the last "major" Negro League. By 1952, most of the young talent in that league was signed into the major leagues, and within a few more years the Negro Leagues became a part of baseball's historical past.

Many Negro Leaguers, including such stars as Robinson, Hank Aaron, Ernie Banks, and Willie Mays, became inducted into the Baseball Hall of Fame as major-league superstars. Their beginnings in the Negro Leagues not only represent a piece of baseball history, but demonstrate the social development of the entire country. Since 1971, several dozen players who achieved success playing largely or entirely in the Negro Leagues also have been voted into the Hall. They have now been given the respect and status that had been denied them during their days on the diamond.

Chapter 2
A Most Valuable Person

Jack Roosevelt Robinson was born on January 31, 1919, just outside of the small town of Cairo in southern Georgia. His parents were Jerry and Mallie Robinson. When Jackie was born, the couple already had three sons (Matthew, Frank, and Edgar) and one daughter (Willa Mae). The new baby's middle name was chosen to honor the former president Teddy Roosevelt, who died just a few weeks earlier, on January 6. Many families like the Robinsons looked up to and admired Roosevelt. The politician was known for promoting equality between Americans, regardless of the color of their skin. At the time, racial inequality and sometimes-violent persecution were widespread. The principle of doing what's right and an awareness of

Mallie Robinson (seated) poses for a family portrait in 1925 with her children (left to right) Matthew (Mack), Jackie, Edgar, Willa Mae, and Frank.

racial injustice were instilled into Jackie from the time he was old enough to understand the difference between right and wrong. His family could not have known how critical a role he would go on to play in creating equal rights for Americans of any color.

Shaped by Slavery

In the early 1900s, the United States was a country shaped by its history of slavery. Slavery was officially abolished in 1865 with the end of the Civil War, the return of Southern states that had seceded from the Union and formed the Confederacy, and the adoption of the Fourteenth Amendment to the U.S. Constitution. After the war, however, many Southern states passed laws legalizing several forms of segregation on the basis of race. These laws, known as Jim Crow laws, reflected attitudes that did not die easily among many whites following the war. The laws also encouraged those attitudes. This meant that African-Americans would be victimized by racial prejudice and persecution well beyond the Civil War.

At the beginning of the 20th century, Jerry and Mallie Robinson were sharecroppers living in southern Georgia. Sharecropping was a type of farming. Sharecroppers lived on land owned by someone else in return for working the land to produce crops and raise livestock. Sharecropping seemed like a good idea, particularly for African-Americans who could not afford to own their own land. But it was often abused and became a way for whites to prevent blacks from gaining an economic advantage now that they were no longer slaves.

RACIAL SEGREGATION AND JIM CROW LAWS

Although slavery had been outlawed since 1865, the segregation, or separation, of Americans based on race was widespread during Jackie Robinson's childhood. Most African-Americans lived under conditions that kept them in poverty, restricted their voting rights, and denied them decent homes, jobs, and educations. Many were also victims of intimidation and violence at the hands of racist groups such as the Ku Klux Klan and other whites who were determined to keep blacks "in their place."

In the South and other former slave-holding areas, so-called Jim Crow laws made segregation legal. African-Americans weren't allowed to attend the same schools, use the same restrooms, or drink from the same water fountains as whites. Movie theaters, concert halls, and restaurants were either completely segregated as to race or had separate seating areas within the same buildings. Similarly, buses had "colored" sections in the back.

In the Northeast, Midwest, and West, African-Americans were also subject to segregation, and black Americans across the country generally had fewer rights and opportunities than white Americans. In many cities outside the South, segregation was not the law, but it was widespread nonetheless. Called "de facto segregation" because it existed not by "law" but "in fact," it developed as African Americans migrated out of the South in search of jobs and a better way of life.

In 1954, the U.S. Supreme Court ruled that segregation was illegal in education. All other segregation laws, such as Jim Crow laws, were abolished under the Civil Rights Act of 1964 and the Voting Rights Act of 1965.

A sign for the "colored" waiting room at the bus station in Durham, North Carolina, in 1940.

SHARECROPPING: A MIXED BAG

After the abolition of slavery, many white landowners suddenly found themselves without slaves to work their land. But many of the recently freed slaves were still there, so sharecropping and other similar arrangements were quickly developed. In Georgia and other Southern states, the African-American population was high. In most cases, land was owned by white families and worked by black families. Under the sharecropping system, landowners had to buy the vegetables or meat produced by their tenants, but the owners could set the prices. These same owners would often operate stores that sold household items. Many owners charged their tenants more money for rent and for items at the store than they paid for crops and livestock. As a result, many sharecroppers traded a life under slavery for one of poverty from which there was little chance of escape.

A family of sharecroppers chops weeds on a cotton field in Georgia in 1941.

Mallie and Jerry

Despite making African-Americans dependent on the whites whose land they were working, sometimes sharecropping actually helped black families survive and live reasonable lives. Jackie's parents struggled with the system and had their share of challenges, but in many ways they succeeded. A large part of that success came from the actions of Jackie's mother, Mallie.

Mallie was one of 14 children. With her many siblings, she grew up on land owned by her parents. Mallie's parents had been born into slavery and were freed when slavery was abolished following the Civil War. They believed in God, education, and hard work, and they made sure their children grew up with those same values. Mallie was able to attend school until the sixth grade, a rare opportunity for a black child at the time. She grew up to be a strong, proud, and kindhearted woman who worked tirelessly to create a happy life for her family. Because of her unique upbringing and education, Mallie always stuck to her ideals, even when times were hard.

Mallie met and married Jerry when she was 14 and he was 18. She fell in love with him, and despite her parent's protest at the marriage, she left her family's land to live with him in a small cabin on the plantation where he had been born and raised. Jerry had grown up working the land and couldn't read or write. His young wife used her education and fierce spirit to help fight Jim Sasser, the plantation owner, for a sharecropping arrangement that was fair. After several hard years, they were earning a decent living, but Jerry wasn't happy with farming or family life.

When Jackie was born, Jerry and Mallie were struggling to keep their marriage together. Jerry had left his wife and kids several times already. With the birth of Jackie, their fifth child, Jerry

The Ku Klux Klan used lynchings, attacks on people's homes and businesses, as well as cross burnings and marches, to harm, intimidate, and kill blacks, Jews, and other minorities. Their tactics were mostly felt in the South, but they made their presence known throughout the nation. This photo, taken around 1920, shows a group of hooded Klansmen at a rally of 30,000 KKK members and their supporters in northern Illinois.

was increasingly restless. He'd been having an affair, and Mallie was fed up. She had forgiven him before, but when he once again left his wife and children just six months after Jackie was born, Mallie knew that something had to change. Jerry eventually came back begging for forgiveness, but this time she said no.

Jim Sasser heard about this, and to spite Mallie, he moved her and her children a few times into smaller and smaller cabins. At the same time, the Ku Klux Klan (KKK), a violent, racist organization based in nearby Atlanta, had been harassing, attacking, and killing black people. Mallie had had enough with the South. Her half-brother had recently told her about a better life in California, and she saw a way out. Together with other members of her extended family, she and her five children made plans to leave Georgia and move to California. On May 21, 1920, Mallie boarded a train bound for Pasadena.

A Pasadena Childhood

When she and her children arrived in Pasadena, Mallie had just a few dollars. She quickly found regular work as a maid for a white family who paid her a decent wage. The Robinson children were all sent to school, and the family tried to settle into life in California. California was not the rural South, but various forms of racial prejudice were nonetheless a fact of everyday life.

Pasadena was a wealthy city with a largely white population. As in most of the nation, its smaller black population was generally segregated from whites and lived in poverty. Blacks didn't have to live under the Jim Crow laws that officially segregated blacks from whites in the South. In Pasadena, however, having dark skin usually meant you would be restricted as to where you could go and what you could do.

Being a minority in a community with a fair amount of racial tension bubbling beneath the surface wasn't an easy way for Jackie to grow up. But Mallie taught her children that the color of their skin didn't determine their worth as human beings. A deeply religious woman who lived by principles she had learned from the Bible, she also taught them to turn the other cheek, to not make things worse by fighting back.

As the first black family on Pepper Street, the Robinsons experienced all kinds of prejudice, from minor insults to physical conflicts. Mallie believed that many negative actions and attitudes toward African-Americans came from ignorance, not cruelty. She had a winning personality, and was a kind and generous woman who spent time, energy, and even money helping others. The more people in the community got to know her, the more they grew used to her and her family.

In school, all of the Robinson kids' teachers and most of their classmates were white. Jackie wasn't a star pupil, but he studied well, and he was well liked by his teachers. Jackie was a natural at sports who always wanted to win,

"Many times I felt that my mother was being foolish, letting people take advantage of her. I was wrong. She did kindness for people whom I considered parasites because she wanted to help them. It was her way of thinking, her way of life."

Jackie Robinson

and thanks to his natural athletic ability, he usually did.

When the financial crisis known as the Great Depression hit the nation in the early 1930s, jobs and money became hard to find. The black population was hit hardest, as white families could no longer afford to pay for help around the house, one of the main sources of employment in the segregated community. To help his mother bring extra money in, the young Jackie performed odd jobs around the neighborhood. Later in his life, Jackie remembered being acutely aware, as a child, that he was a minority, that he was poorer than most kids at his school, and that unlike most of his peers, he didn't have a father. Mallie never remarried, and Jerry never re-entered her life or the lives of the children.

A Sporting Chance

As he entered his teenage years, Jackie became even more involved in sports. In 1935, after completing junior high, Jackie started attending John Muir Technical High School, or Muir Tech. The high school was known for its competitive sports programs, and Jackie earned the position of shortstop on the baseball team. He also ran track and competed in the long jump and high jump, played on the basketball team, was a strong tennis player, and later joined the football team.

Jackie's brother Matthew, who was known as "Mack" to everyone, was also a natural athlete. Mack excelled at track and field. He was a powerful runner and gifted at the long jump. When the Olympics came to Los Angeles

THE 1936 BERLIN OLYMPICS:
CONTROVERSY ON THE WORLD STAGE

The Berlin Olympics, in which Jackie Robinson's older brother Mack competed, were controversial for several reasons. In 1931, when Berlin, Germany, was chosen as the site of the 1936 Olympics, the Nazis, under the leadership of Adolf Hitler, had not yet risen to power. Hitler became the nation's chancellor, or leader, in 1933, and by 1936 the Nazis' horrific campaign to rid Europe of many of its racial and ethnic minorities, Jews in particular, was in its early stages.

During the run-up to the Olympics, a debate swirled as to whether participating in the Games would be seen as an endorsement of the Nazis' racist beliefs. The Nazis had already put into effect many anti-Semitic, or anti-Jewish, laws in Germany, and it was only under threat of an international boycott of the Games that Hitler finally agreed to allow Jews and blacks from other nations to compete in Germany.

At the Games, African-American sprinter and long jumper Jesse Owens took four gold medals, including one in the 200-meter sprint, where he narrowly beat Mack Robinson, who placed second and took the silver medal.

Owens' victories were considered a slap in the face of Hitler and his using the Olympics to showcase Nazi ideals of racial superiority. Hitler was widely reported to have refused to shake hands with any of the black athletes who competed, including Jesse Owens and Mack Robinson. According to some reports, when told by international Olympic officials that he should acknowledge all of the winners regardless of race, or none, Hitler chose to acknowledge none.

Adolf Hitler (second from right) and other leaders of Nazi Germany watch the 1936 Berlin Olympics. Jesse Owens' four gold medals flew in the face of Hitler's plan to use the Games to promote Nazi ideals of white racial superiority.

in 1932, Mack was inspired by the incredible array of international athletes. He dedicated himself to training, working hard not only to become a top-flight athlete but also to make his own way through the ranks despite the added hardship of competing at a time when few favors were granted to black athletes. At last, he earned a place on the 1936 U.S. Olympic team, traveling to Germany to compete in the Berlin Olympics. There, with his family listening on the radio back in Pasadena, Mack won the silver medal in the 200-meter sprint. He was second to Jesse Owens, another African-American athlete, who set an Olympic record with his time of 20.7 seconds.

Jesse Owens at the start of his medal-winning performance in the 200-meter sprint at the 1936 Berlin Olympics.

Four Letters

Back at home, the teenaged Jackie was also becoming an admired athlete. He played tennis competitively, and even though he didn't practice often, he won several regional tournaments. At Muir Tech, he earned varsity letters in four sports: track and field, basketball, football, and baseball. "Lettering" in sports means that you are awarded the right to wear an emblem, usually the initial of the school, on a special sweater or jacket. Receiving a letter was a big accomplishment. Earning four in one year was almost unheard of. Unlike his brother Mack, who was primarily an athlete in solo sports, Jackie was a great team player. His desire to win was so strong that he never sought to steal the limelight. "It kills me to lose," he once said. "That's the way I am about winning, all I ever wanted to do was finish first."

In 1937, following his graduation from Muir Tech, the 18-year-old Jackie enrolled at Pasadena Junior College (PJC). PJC was a college linked to Muir, and tuition was free. For the Robinsons, free college was a godsend. Mack was already enrolled at PJC when Jackie arrived. As a star sprinter and Olympic athlete, the older Robinson was held in awe by the student population and local newspapers. While Jackie was obviously talented at sports, he was overshadowed at PJC by his brother's exploits. But he didn't seem to mind. While Jackie was intensely competitive, he wasn't trying to compete with his brother.

In his first year at PJC, Jackie continued to mold his legacy in sports, playing tennis, basketball, baseball, and football, as well as somehow finding time to compete in track and field. On the baseball diamond, he was a solid shortstop, but it was in his performance at the plate and on the bases that his talent really started to shine. He had an incredible knack for stealing bases. His speed and daring caught the attention of everyone who watched him play. In nearly every game, he stole at least one base. His exploits were fun to watch and earned him the respect of his teammates, coaches, and fans.

His speed helped him excel in other sports, too. When Jackie started playing football for PJC, he was quickly recognized as a force to be reckoned with. In September 1937, he became the quarterback for the PJC Bulldogs. Early in the season, he chipped a bone in his leg and was unable to play for another month, but when he returned, he played better than ever. He passed brilliantly and ran numerous plays on his own, often running the ball for touchdowns.

The next year, Mack left Pasadena Junior College to enroll at Oregon State University, propelling Jackie into the role of PJC's star athlete. At a track and field meet that school year, he won the long jump with an amazing leap of 25 feet, 6.5 inches (nearly 8 meters). It broke his brother's longstanding school record and set a national junior college record. On the same day, he played baseball for the PJC team. Just a week earlier, he had been named the Most Valuable Player in the region for baseball. He also had an amazing football season with the Bulldogs, leading the team to 11 wins and no losses, scoring 17 touchdowns, and creating countless amazing plays. At the end of the season, he was named the region's Most Valuable Player.

Moving On

Although he was quickly becoming a local sports hero, Jackie still faced racial prejudice in nearly every facet of his life. As in high school, most of the people on the field or court were white, and cruel comments and racial slurs

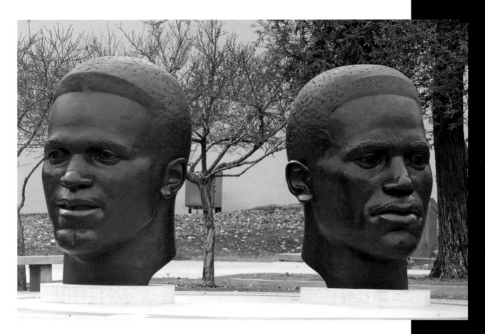

The silver medal-winning performance of Jackie Robinson's older brother Mack at the 1936 Olympics, while outstanding, couldn't compare to teammate Jesse Owens' four gold medals. In the years just after the Olympics, Mack held a variety of low-paying jobs to support his young family. Later, he worked with troubled youth, fighting against street crime in Pasadena. Eventually, he received the recognition he deserved. At the 1984 Los Angeles Olympics, he was chosen to help carry the Olympic flag at the opening ceremonies. And in 1997, both he and Jackie were honored by the city of Pasadena with this statue outside City Hall (Jackie on left, Mack on right). Mack died in March 2000 at the age of 85.

were common. Jackie and his friends mostly took these experiences in stride, but the more he experienced them, the less he liked being in Pasadena. As he grew older, he became increasingly disturbed by the bigotry and prejudice he experienced.

A 1982 U.S. "Black Heritage" postage stamp honors the life and legacy of Jackie Robinson. Even as a young athlete in high school, junior college, and college, two standards guided Jackie's performance: being on the playing field rather than watching from the sidelines, and playing to win.

In the 1930s, California still experienced widespread racial segregation, and Jim Crow-like laws meant that he and his friends and family could only eat at certain restaurants, sit in "colored" sections at movie theaters, and ride in the back of buses. In early 1939, his oldest brother Edgar was wrongfully stopped and beaten up by the Pasadena police. The event made Jackie bitter about the town he had grown up in. Jackie himself had had run-ins with the Pasadena police during his teenage years and was even sentenced to ten days in jail at one point. It was for an incident that stemmed from Jackie and a friend singing a popular song while walking home one night. A police officer stopped the two boisterous singers in the street and was ready to detain Jackie's friend, but Jackie loudly protested.

Jackie argued with the policeman, and the situation quickly got out of hand. By sticking up for his friend, he earned himself a night in custody and a ten-day jail sentence. The sentence was suspended, but it didn't sit well with him. Jackie was known for having a temper and a strong sense of right and wrong. He was never afraid to speak his mind to anyone, police included, and it sometimes got him into trouble. He occasionally got into fights, sometimes even while playing sports.

At the end of his second year at PJC, Jackie was ready to leave Pasadena. Because he was such an amazing athlete, many top schools were interested in him. He was offered a few athletic scholarships, but some of the schools only accepted black students to give the impression of equality. Many schools had policies that didn't allow black students at all, and others would accept African-Americans as part of their athletic programs, but never allow them to actively participate. Jackie didn't want to sit on a bench somewhere; he wanted to play.

After talking through his options with his brother Frank, a soft-spoken, gentle man who always looked out for his little brother, Jackie decided on the University of California, Los Angeles (UCLA). UCLA offered Jackie an athletic scholarship, and it was close by, so Jackie could commute and Frank could come to watch him compete. UCLA's athletic program wasn't as strong as some of the other schools that were interested in him, but if he went to UCLA, he'd be on the playing field, not watching from the sidelines. And to Jackie, that was what mattered. As he said later:

"Life is not a spectator sport. If you're going to spend your whole life in the grandstand just watching what goes on, in my opinion you're wasting your life."

Chapter 3
Fighting a Battle on the Home Front

Jackie started at UCLA on February 15, 1939. Most people who knew Jackie, or had heard about his abilities, expected him to try out for tennis, baseball, basketball, and football, as he had done at Muir Tech and Pasadena Junior College. But Jackie announced that he would only join the UCLA football and track teams. He said he wanted to study, but most people saw through that. Jackie wanted to follow in his brother Mack's footsteps and compete in the 1940 Olympics. The events of the year that followed would change Jackie's plans and the course of his life forever.

Trying Times

Jackie began the year strong, studying as promised and engaging only lightly in sports. But on July 10, 1939, Frank Robinson was hit by a car while he was riding his motorcycle. He died just hours after being rushed to the hospital. Jackie was devastated by the loss of his brother and turned once again to sports.

Before he could get over this family tragedy, his focus was again shaken, this time by another incident with police. In September, Jackie and some of his friends were driving home when they found themselves involved in

When Jackie Robinson first enrolled at UCLA in 1939, he said he would limit his involvement in sports. Within a year or two, however, he had become an outstanding athlete in four sports.

Jackie Robinson as an all-conference back in 1940. Jackie resented the unwanted preferential treatment he received as a star member of the UCLA football team.

an incident with a white man who called them racist names. The confrontation ended without violence, but a passing Pasadena police officer stopped to disperse a crowd that had gathered. Most people who were there left before the officer could make any arrests, but Jackie stayed and argued with the officer.

The officer pulled his gun on Jackie and arrested him. Jackie was jailed overnight, pleaded "not guilty" to trumped-up charges of "hindering traffic" and "resisting arrest," and was released on bail. Without Jackie's knowledge, Jackie's UCLA coach and other prominent people, many of them UCLA Bruins fans, arranged a deal to change his "not guilty" plea to "guilty." As part of this deal, he would not serve any additional jail time. Jackie later found out that his plea had been changed without his consent, and that people working on his behalf did so out of concern for the football team and not because the charges were unjust.

Jackie was angry that he would not have the chance to fight the charges on his own. He was disturbed by the bigotry that was at the core of his arrest and by the fact that his being spared jail time did nothing to address the injustices that black people were subjected to every day. He knew it was his athletic ability that had saved him from jail time, and this only made him feel more fully the weight of being a member of a persecuted minority.

Staying Busy and Focused

When the 1940 Olympics were canceled following Nazi Germany's invasion of Poland in 1939 and the start of World War II in Europe, Jackie settled into academic life and changed his mind about competing only in football and track. First he joined the basketball team and then the baseball team, making him once again a four-letter athlete, UCLA's first.

Jackie and Rachel: A Love Story

In early 1941, Jackie met a 17-year-old UCLA student from Los Angeles named Rachel Annetta Isum. Rachel's father, Charles, had been a bookbinder for the *Los Angeles Times*, but was forced into early retirement by severe health problems he developed after being gassed during service in World War I. Her mom, Zellee, was a self-employed caterer who was grooming her daughter to follow in her footsteps.

Rachel Isum in January 1946, at the age of 23.

When Rachel met Jackie, she was self-conscious about her appearance. She worried about her hair and felt her brown skin was too dark, although it was much lighter than Jackie's. Jackie, on the other hand, had no hang-ups about his body or skin. He constantly wore white shirts, which emphasized the darkness of his skin. As Rachel later recalled:

"He wore his color with such dignity and pride and confidence that after a little while I didn't even think about it. He was never, ever, ashamed of his color."

After meeting on campus, Jackie and Rachel started spending more and more time together. Rachel was studious and intended to go into nursing, but Jackie was falling behind on his schoolwork. His focus was on athletics. He did tell her he wanted to coach at the university level, which would have meant earning a degree, but he seemed to care more about playing sports than he did about studying.

Charles was, like most fathers, reluctant to see his daughter dating an older man. But Zellee loved Jackie and made him feel welcome. At the Robinson house, Rachel was also made to feel welcome. Jackie's brothers and sister all liked her, and Mallie saw in her the perfect partner for her son—a polite, religious girl who had goals of her own. "Everything that she would have wanted for Jack—that was me," Rachel recalled.

Their relationship developed slowly. Despite being handsome and athletic, Jackie could be shy and uncertain. He was also deeply committed to his physical health as an athlete and would never stay awake later than midnight. Rachel later admitted that this had a pretty big impact on their ability to do things together. But the couple, as they were starting to be viewed on campus, liked each other a lot. In November, Jackie took Rachel to a homecoming dance at a fancy Los Angeles hotel. They dressed for the occasion, Jackie in his only suit and Rachel in a new dress and fur coat that had been her grandmother's. They were awkward, but it was a sweet first date, and Rachel would remember it fondly. "I really wanted him to kiss me," she said.

"He pecked me on the cheek. That was all. I was disappointed." But her disappointment was short-lived, and she and Jackie continued to see each other over the coming months.

In Search of a Path

The early part of 1941 was challenging in many ways. Jackie's grades were slipping, and his faith in varsity sports was starting to slip. Jackie was considered one of the country's best college football players. He had played well for UCLA the previous season, but the team as a whole had done poorly, finishing with only one win against nine losses. On the basketball court, it was a similar story. Jackie was regularly touted as the team's best player, but the team itself had a 6–20 overall record. And at various ceremonies, he was passed over for awards. There was speculation that these omissions were racially based.

With little hope of succeeding at a career in business due to the color of his skin, and with even less hope of entering professional sports, which were almost entirely segregated, Jackie found the prospect of staying at UCLA unappealing. Also, Mallie was struggling financially and Jackie wanted to help her out. This gave him another reason for leaving school. But what could he do instead?

At the time, the National Football League (NFL) was whites-only. In 1941, the overwhelming majority of pro basketball teams were all white, with a few all-black teams sprinkled around. And of course, professional baseball was still strictly segregated between the all-white major leagues and the all-black

Negro Leagues. Without a clear idea of what he would do next, he made up his mind. In March 1941, against the protests of Rachel, his mother, and his coaches, and just months shy of graduation, Jackie officially arranged for his "honorable dismissal" from the university.

Meanwhile, he and Rachel were growing closer. Jackie sent her a charm bracelet hung with the tiny footballs, basketballs, and baseballs he had received for his participation with various teams over the years. It wasn't an engagement ring, but it was a sign of his commitment. She wore it proudly. When her father passed away shortly after Jackie left UCLA, Rachel turned to him for support. Jackie later recalled that the depth of Rachel's grief had "a profound effect" on him:

> *"I knew that our relationship was to be one of the most important things in my life no matter what happened to me."*

As for Rachel, she realized that the death of her dad "gave Jack [who had grown up without a father of his own] an opening where he could at last be the man, the main man, in a family of his own."

Adios, California

After leaving UCLA, and still without a clear career path ahead of him, Jackie took a temporary job as an assistant athletic director at a government-sponsored youth camp in California. After the camp closed in the summer of 1941, Jackie was selected to play with an all-star college-level football team in an annual charity game against the Chicago Bears of the NFL.

In the fall of 1941, Jackie was offered a position with the Honolulu Bears, A racially integrated semi-professional team, in Hawaii. The offer included a contract to work construction in Pearl Harbor, which meant he'd be able to send money home to help Mallie. There, Jackie played good football and was popular in the newspapers, but he wasn't the best worker. Manual labor had never been his strong suit. He was muscular and athletic, but he didn't seem to apply the same energy to work as he did on the field. After a short stint in Honolulu, Jackie decided to go back home. He formally resigned from the team, quit his job, and packed his bags. On December 7, 1941, while he was on a ship headed back to California, Japan attacked Pearl Harbor, and the United States was officially at war.

When Jackie got home, he couldn't settle into a normal life. He joined the Los Angeles Bulldogs, an integrated team in a high-level minor football league, but he suffered a mild ankle injury in the first game of the season. Between that and the United States going to war, his brief career in pro football came to a halt. The U.S. government had begun building up its military, and Jackie was faced with the increasing likelihood of being drafted into the Army, despite his persistent ankle injury. He wanted to do his part in fighting against the evils of Japan and its military partner, Nazi Germany, but Jackie knew the military had a long history of segregation and discrimination. When he received a notice of induction into

An African-American military policeman (MP) in front of a "colored" MP entrance during World War II.

the Army, however, he didn't feel he had much of a choice. On April 3, 1942, Jackie Robinson showed up for service and was sent to Fort Riley, Kansas, for basic training.

Fighting Two Wars

About the time that Jackie was drafted, there was a huge increase in the number of black men enlisting in the U.S. Army. The fact that both Germany and Japan were invading and taking over vast portions of the globe motivated many Americans to serve, and African Americans were no exception. The full extent of the horror of the Nazis' persecuting, enslaving, and murdering millions of European Jews, Poles, and other groups was not yet realized. Still, African Americans had witnessed the racial politics and practices of Hitler and the Nazis during and since the 1936 Berlin Olympics.

At the same time, many black Americans were reminded during World War II of an unofficial battle they were fighting for freedom, equality, and full rights at home. Certainly, the fight against oppression and cruelty abroad was a worthwhile cause. During basic training, however, Jackie experienced firsthand the fact that racial discrimination and tensions were as deeply ingrained in the U.S. military as they were in everyday American life. The Army was completely segregated by race and insisted that a white officer be in charge of every black unit. Jackie's athleticism and intelligence set him apart from many of his fellow recruits, white and black alike, but when he applied for Officer Candidate School (OCS), he was refused and assigned instead to look after horses in the

AFRICAN AMERICANS IN WORLD WAR II

Before World War II, just a few thousand African Americans were enlisted in the U.S. armed forces. As the need for soldiers to fight in World War II increased, this number soared. Pressure from politicians and civil rights activists led to military organizations easing their restrictions on African-American enlistment. But Jim Crow rules within the military meant that many African-American servicemen were forced into tasks like cooking, cleaning, or driving, rather than the active fighting for which they were trained.

Segregation in the military included separate living quarters, washrooms, mess halls, and even segregated units. Only a small percentage of African-American soldiers actually saw combat, mostly in the later stages of the war, and most, if not all, faced harsh discrimination on a daily basis. As the war progressed, African-American men showed their courage in battle. Segregated units like the Tuskegee Airmen (the 99th Fighter Squadron of the U.S. Army Air Forces and the subjects of the 2012 movie *Red Tails*) and Jackie Robinson's own 761st Tank Battalion earned distinction for their heroic actions in battle. During the Battle of the Bulge in Europe in December 1944, over 2,000 African-American soldiers fought alongside white soldiers in integrated units. Just a few years after the end of the war, President Harry S. Truman ended segregation in the armed forces.

Several Tuskegee Airmen, the first group of African-American military aviators in the U.S. armed forces, are shown at a mission briefing in Italy in 1945.

stables. He was even turned away when he tried to join the Fort Riley baseball team.

During basic training at Fort Riley, Jackie met boxer Joe Louis, who was the current world heavyweight champion. Joe had joined the Army voluntarily in January 1942, and the two became friends. They played golf together, and Jackie even joined Joe in boxing training sessions. Joe learned about the trouble Jackie and other young black soldiers were having getting their OCS applications processed. Joe was not afraid to use his celebrity status and his connections with people in the U.S. government to stir things up and champion the cause of Jackie and his fellow soldiers. In November of 1942, the Army finally eased back on their restrictions and considered the applications of African-Americans to OCS.

Advancing … Up to a Point

Jackie joined a group of 80 individuals, white and black, in a 13-week training session. The program was fully integrated. The soldiers all studied, ate, trained, and lived together. On January 28, 1943, Jackie earned the rank of second lieutenant. He was given a brief leave of absence, and he traveled back to California. Rachel was now living in San Francisco, studying nursing. Decked out in his formal cavalry officer's uniform, Jackie found her and immediately proposed marriage. She accepted.

After a few days with his new fiancée, Jackie headed back to Fort Riley. There, he was assigned to be morale officer to an all-black battalion at the base. This meant that his job was to help keep up the spirits, self-confidence, and enthusiasm of the soldiers in his unit. As to keeping up his own morale, Jackie stayed in touch with his buddy Joe Louis, with whom he continued to play golf. He also took up table tennis, which he had dabbled in as a younger

Joe Louis: World Champ and National Hero

When Jackie Robinson met Joe Louis in basic training in 1942, Louis was the world heavyweight champion. He was also, at a time when racial discrimination was still legal in many parts of the nation, a genuine hero to Americans of every race, religion, color, and background. In 1938, he had defended his title against Max Schmeling, a German boxer who had become yet another tool in the Nazis' campaign to promote the superiority of Germany and the white race. Joe became, in a sense, the face of Americans' increasing hatred of the Nazis in the years leading up to World War II. The fact that he was a black man in the 1930s and 1940s made his rise not only among African Americans but into the world of boxing, and beyond, even more remarkable. Joe had not only defeated the Nazis' "poster child" for German racial supremacy, but he fought several bouts in 1942 to raise money for the U.S. war effort.

Between these fights, Joe had voluntarily enlisted in the Army. As a private, he lent his face, name, uniform, and words to support the war effort. In one exchange, he famously responded to a question about his willingness to become a member of the segregated U.S. Army: "Lots of things wrong with America, but Hitler ain't going to fix them."

man. He entered and won a table-tennis competition that made him the top Ping-Pong player in the Army.

Jackie's unit, like other African-American units, was not being asked to fight, though, even though the war was intensifying overseas. The Army now allowed black men to become officers, and it was certainly willing to accept thousands upon thousands of black recruits. Racist policies and attitudes were so deeply rooted throughout the military, however, that the Army stood by its long-held refusal to send African-Americans into battle. Black soldiers were being trained in combat, and they were being sent overseas. Rather than being allowed to assume the responsibilities and risks, and to share the glory, of fighting on the field of battle, however, they were assigned to service units that helped feed, supply, and transport combat units.

At Fort Riley, segregation was worse than ever. Jackie was once again refused a spot on the baseball team. He was asked to join the football team, but he quit when other bases refused to play Fort Riley on the grounds that they had a black player on their team. Across the country, even as the military was fighting racism and oppression overseas, racial tensions were running higher than ever. In some parts of the country, black servicemen were being harassed, attacked, and in some cases killed off base by white civilians and law enforcement personnel. As morale officer to a group of black soldiers serving a deeply segregated nation in a deeply segregated Army, Jackie was kept busy. His position with the men wasn't helped by the fact that his own feelings were so conflicted about his role in the military.

Around this time, Jackie's spirits hit another low when he and Rachel ended their engagement over an argument. In early 1944, Rachel had decided to join the Nurse Cadet Corps. Women were joining similar service outfits and entering the workforce as part of the war effort, and Rachel herself worked nights in an aircraft factory. Still, Jackie did not want her to join the Corps. He felt that her being in the service would offer too many temptations for her to cheat on him. He told her she had to either leave the Corps or leave him. Jackie's distrust and stubborn, opinionated nature had pushed the deeply committed Rachel to break up with him.

Earning Respect

Jackie's temper was known not only to those closest to him, but to the people he served with in the Army. He was also known for his intelligence and ability to handle himself well under pressure. It didn't take long for others to recognize his abilities as a soldier and an officer, and on April 13, 1944, he was transferred to Camp Hood (present-day Fort Hood), Texas, to head up an all-black tank battalion. Jackie had been trained as a cavalry officer, and his experience was with horses, not tanks. He admitted in front of the entire group of soldiers that he knew nothing about tank warfare and allowed a sergeant to lead the unit instead. This kind of honesty earned him the respect of his men.

While he wasn't leading the battalion anymore, Jackie was still morale officer and

U.S. troops advance into a town in Belgium in 1944 under the protection of a heavy tank.

A U.S. Army machine-gunner assigned to a tank in France, as photographed in 1944. It was around this time that all-black tank battalions, like the one to which Jackie was assigned, were being shipped overseas to fight in Europe.

showed excellent leadership skills in other ways. He organized baseball and softball games that boosted morale among the men and kept them busy, even though he couldn't fully participate himself. His ankle had been injured and re-injured several times both on the playing field and during combat training.

When it looked as if his battalion was actually going to be sent overseas to join in the fighting, he was given a medical exam to see if he was fit for service. The X-rays showed chips of bone loose inside his ankle, but he was still approved for limited service overseas. Before he could ship out, however, he became embroiled in an incident that showed his determination to stand up to racism—and landed him in serious trouble.

The Back of the Bus

On July 6, 1944, Jackie was riding a military bus back to Camp Hood from a nearby hospital, where he was being treated for his ankle injury. Just a month earlier, the Army had officially banned segregation on military buses. Times were changing, however slowly, but it would take more than changes in military procedure to put an end to racial prejudice. On his way toward the back of the bus, where until recently, all African-American soldiers were required to sit, Jackie saw a woman he knew, the wife of a fellow officer. He sat next to her, at the middle of the bus. The driver stopped and ordered him to the back. Jackie refused.

The exchange became heated, and eventually the military police (MPs) were called in. The incident became chaotic, with multiple versions being told to the MPs. Jackie was taken into custody, but his battalion commander, a white man, refused to issue charges against him.

A few weeks later, Jackie was transferred to a new battalion, where the commander didn't know him and agreed to a criminal trial known in the military as a court-martial. Jackie was placed under arrest and charged with a host of offenses, including drunkenness (even though he didn't drink), insubordination, and "willful disobedience" toward a commanding officer.

Jackie's lawyers took several approaches to his defense. On a subjective, or personal, level, they attempted to show that he had been treated with disrespect as both an officer and a human being on the bus and after he had been taken into custody. When it came to establishing the actual facts of the incident and its aftermath, the court case was confusing and full of conflicting testimony. His lawyers, however, were able to provide evidence of Jackie's solid reputation as an officer. They also showed that while he wasn't completely innocent of provocative behavior, most of his behavior was appropriate to the situation and he had broken no Army rules that would lead to a court-martial.

During the trial, Jackie himself testified and gave a moving speech about slavery and his indignation at being called a "nigger" by the military personnel and civilians involved after he had been taken into custody. He talked about the definition of the word:

"It was a small victory, for I had learned that I was in two wars, one against the foreign enemy, the other against prejudice at home."

Jackie Robinson, on the outcome of his court-martial

"I looked it up once, but my grandmother gave me a good definition. She was a slave and she said the definition of the word was a low, uncouth person, and pertains to no one in particular. But I don't consider that I am low and uncouth. I objected to being called a nigger.... I told the Captain, I said, 'If you call me a nigger, I might have to say the same thing to you. I do not consider myself a nigger at all. I am a negro, but not a nigger."

Even then, before he became a hero to millions on the baseball diamond, people saw in Jackie Robinson a remarkable courage, strength of character, and intelligence. He was, for many, a bright example of a black man who refused to back down and be treated as anything less than a person with the same rights as anyone else. He was a man who knew his worth as a human being. Mallie had taught him that. Before the case against Jackie came to trial, several of the charges were dropped, and when the trial finally wrapped up four hours after it began, he was found "not guilty of all specifications and charges."

Back to Baseball

Although the court-martial had gone his way, Jackie was now thinking of life outside the military. Between his nagging ankle injury and the shadow that his court case cast over his military career, he was ready to return to civilian life. He requested retirement from active service. It took time to process, but he was eventually granted an honorable discharge based on his injury on November 28, 1944. At around the same time, following the advice of his mother, he finally swallowed his pride and contacted Rachel again. They were able to end their disagreement and resume their engagement.

Jackie Robinson in late 1944 or early 1945, signing military papers around the time of his discharge from the Army based on a chronic ankle injury.

Just before leaving the Army, Jackie looked into the current state of the Negro Leagues. Fan attendance was growing. Players were finally beginning to earn a decent wage. And most importantly, with so many African-Americans serving in the military, the leagues needed players.

A former pitcher for the Kansas City Monarchs, one of the most famous Negro League teams, suggested that Jackie contact co-owner Thomas Y. Baird. Jackie sent Baird a letter, and after some negotiation, he was offered an opportunity to try out for the team the following spring. If he made the team, he'd be paid $400 a month.

Jackie showed up at the Monarchs' spring training camp in Houston, Texas, in April 1945. Jackie was humble and modest, and he worked as hard as any other players in camp. He didn't

Jackie Robinson with the Kansas City Monarchs in 1945.

put on any airs about being a star. It had, after all, been years since he played baseball at UCLA. He made the team and started traveling with the Monarchs around the country. Jackie quickly realized what it meant to play in the Negro Leagues. They traveled in old, uncomfortable buses and stayed in dirty Jim Crow hotels. They weren't allowed in white restaurants and had to use separate "colored" washrooms, sometimes so disgusting that they were almost unusable. Games were often held at strange hours, sometimes late at night.

Despite all the difficulties, Jackie found himself in the midst of a group of enthusiastic, supportive teammates. He became the team's shortstop and played his position well. He wasn't happy with the quality of life in the Negro Leagues, but he had the same burning desire to win that had driven his life from an early age. That competitive spirit made Jackie's exploits on the field a joy to watch. His season with the Monarchs gave him the opportunity to brush up on old skills and learn new ones. It was an experience that would prove indispensable to his future.

At around the same time, several critics of Jim Crow rules in sports were trying to integrate baseball. Officially, there was no rule that said black players could not enter the major leagues, but the unofficial rules persisted. One person pushing for integration was Wendell

THE KANSAS CITY MONARCHS:
A LEGENDARY NEGRO LEAGUES TEAM

In 1920, a group of African-American baseball teams started playing under the name of the Negro National League (NNL). Andrew "Rube" Foster, the enterprising owner of the Chicago American Giants and a former pitcher, had been trying to form a league consisting of black teams for years. In its opening season, the league had eight teams, including the Kansas City Monarchs, founded earlier that year by white businessman J. L. Wilkinson.

The Monarchs were a strong team and became immediate rivals to Rube Foster's American Giants. The team lost the league championship to Chicago for the first few years, but then Wilkinson replaced his manager with a Cuban player named José Méndez.

In 1924, the NNL hosted the first-ever Colored World Series, pitting its champion team against the top team from the Eastern Colored League. Méndez led the Monarchs to win both the NNL pennant and the Series. They would go on to win a total of ten league championships and, in 1942, a second Colored World Series. In 1930, they became the first baseball team to use portable lighting at night games. The Monarchs were such a solid team, run by a shrewd businessman, that they were able to continue playing when the Depression forced the closure of the Negro National League in 1931. After a few years of playing independently, they joined the newly formed Negro American League in 1937.

Playing in the Negro Leagues involved putting up with discrimination and dealing with Jim Crow laws, but the Monarchs prided themselves on being professional, and players were expected to conduct themselves with dignity. When Jackie Robinson joined the team in 1945, the Monarchs were widely known and respected. Its players at the time, including a talented base stealer who went by the name of "Cool Papa" Bell, were heroes to young black Americans across the country. When they played home games, they often drew more fans than Kansas City's white minor league team.

By the time the team disbanded in 1965, the Monarchs had sent more black players to the major leagues than any other Negro League team. At least 14 players and managers who played with the Kansas City Monarchs are now members of the Baseball Hall of Fame.

Smith, a reporter for the *Pittsburgh Courier*, one of the top black newspapers of its day. Wendell and a Boston city councilman named Isadore Muchnick convinced the major league Boston Red Sox to allow black players to try out for the team. Jackie was invited to the tryout session, along with several other black ballplayers.

While Jackie impressed the Red Sox manager, the session was nothing more than a publicity stunt, staged mostly to keep Muchnick and other anti-segregationists off the team's back. The team never got back to him, and the experience was generally humiliating and frustrating. (The Red Sox would continue to field all-white teams until 1959, 12 years after the color line was erased, making them the last team in the majors to integrate their roster.) Still, the day wasn't entirely wasted. The mere fact of Jackie's appearance at a tryout was an important step toward at least putting the idea of integrated big-league baseball in view. Plus, Wendell Smith would go on to become an important figure in Jackie's professional life.

At the time, Jackie didn't know any of that. He certainly had no idea what changes might

The Kansas City Monarchs, of the Negro National League, and the Hilldale Club, of the Eastern Colored League, line up before the opening of the 1924 Colored World Series.

be coming, or how huge a role he would play in bringing them about. What he did know was that he was sick of segregated baseball and tired of playing and traveling under conditions that were degrading and undignified. Rachel had just graduated with honors from the University of California. She quickly found a good job at Los Angeles General Hospital, and Jackie was planning to quit the Monarchs and look for a job back home as well, as a high school coach.

Before their plans could take shape, however, a man walked onto the field at Comiskey Park, home of the rival Chicago American Giants, and changed Jackie's life forever. The man's name was Clyde Sukeforth. He told Jackie he'd been sent by Branch Rickey, general manager of the Brooklyn Dodgers. Everyone knew Rickey was one of the most influential and outspoken figures in major league baseball at the time. Sukeforth said that Mr. Rickey wanted to meet Jackie. He also asked Jackie to throw a few balls for him, to show off his arm strength.

Jackie listened to the man's questions and then spoke up. "Why is Mr. Rickey interested in my arm? Why is he interested in me?"

SANTOP WINTERS CURRIE LEE CARR C.JOHNSON J.JOHNSON RYAN MACKEY ALLEN CAMPBELL LEWIS THOMAS COCKRELL BRIGGS WARFIELD STEVENS LAMBERT

Chapter 4
Moving Up

On August 28, 1945, Jackie Robinson was in New York City—in the part of New York City known as Brooklyn, to be exact. Sitting in a small office, he was about to get answers to his questions about the Dodgers' sudden interest in him. It was a sweltering summer day. Sitting behind the desk was an almost mythical figure. Branch Rickey was a large man with an air of confidence about him. He wore round glasses and had big, bushy eyebrows. His face was large, square, and expressive, with deep lines etched around his eyes. He was dressed in a suit and bow tie, and he clutched a large cigar. For the first few minutes of their meeting, Rickey just stared at Jackie. Not knowing what else to do, Jackie simply stared back. The room buzzed with anticipation. Finally, Rickey broke the silence. "Do you have a girl?" he asked. Caught off guard, Jackie replied, "I'm not sure." The athlete explained that he was engaged but was worried about his constant traveling and uncertain future. Rickey smiled at him. "You know you have a girl," he said. "When we get through today you may want to call her up because there are times when a man needs a woman by his side."

Branch Rickey and Jackie Robinson agree to terms on a historic one-year contract between Jackie and the Dodger organization for the 1946 baseball season.

The Other Cheek

The president and general manger of the Brooklyn Dodgers told Jackie to marry Rachel because he was going to need all the support he could get. He then asked if Jackie knew why he'd been invited to the meeting. Jackie said he thought Rickey was putting together an all-black team and wanted him to play for it.

"No, that isn't it," said Rickey. "You were brought here, Jackie, to play for the Brooklyn organization. Perhaps on Montreal to start with." Rickey was referring to the Montreal Royals. The Royals, members of the Class-AAA International League, were Brooklyn's top minor-league team. Then, if all went well, he would have a shot at playing for the parent club, the Dodgers. Jackie was silent. "I was thrilled, scared, and excited," he said later. The larger-than-life baseball giant thumped his desk and half shouted. "I want to win the pennant and we need ball players! Do you think you can do it?" Jackie just stared. Finally, after a painfully long time, he said a single word that would ensure his place in history: "Yes."

The meeting wasn't over yet. Rickey wanted to know if Jackie had what it took to be the first black baseball player in the major leagues. It wasn't just about his abilities as a player, he said. He questioned Jackie at length about all the trials he would face as an African-American in the public spotlight. He acted out several role-playing scenarios, challenging Jackie as various bigoted white people he might meet during the course of a career in the majors. He shouted insults at Jackie. He took off his suit jacket and acted convincingly like

> "We can win only if we can convince the world that I'm doing this because you're a great ballplayer and a fine gentleman."
>
> Branch Rickey

the worst racist anyone could imagine. Jackie clenched his hands behind his back.

At one point, posing as a white ballplayer furious at being tagged out by a black player, Rickey even faked a punch at Jackie. Rickey insisted that Jackie could never hit back, yell, or argue. If he did, Rickey said, the whole "experiment" would end badly. He kept asking, "What would you do?" Finally, after putting up with abuse for almost an hour, Jackie asked the Dodgers' manager, "Mr. Rickey, do you want a ballplayer who's afraid to fight back?" Rickey responded instantly, "I want a ballplayer with guts enough to not fight back!"

Jackie agreed that he was up to the task. They talked about the Biblical principle of turning the other cheek when faced with aggression or discrimination. "Mr. Rickey, I've got two cheeks," said Jackie. Satisfied with the response, Branch Rickey offered Jackie Robinson a contract with the Brooklyn Dodgers organization.

A few months later, in late October, they made the news public. When reporters asked Jackie for his thoughts, he said, "I can't begin to tell you how happy I am that I am the first member of my race in organized baseball," he said. "I realize how much it means to me, my race, and to baseball. I can only say I'll do my very best to come through in every manner." Rickey was later interviewed about signing Jackie and his announcement that his scouts had found 25 black ballplayers he was considering bringing up to the major leagues. He said, "I have never meant to be a crusader and I hope I won't be regarded as one.

My purpose is to be fair to all people, and my selfish objective is to win baseball games."

After a whirlwind season of winter ball in Venezuela, Jackie returned to California to prepare for his wedding. He was nervous, but excited. On February 10, 1946, after a five-year engagement, Rachel Annetta Isum became Rachel Robinson, Jackie's wife. Now husband and wife, the happy couple nervously prepared for what was going to come.

Jackie and Rachel are married on February 10, 1946, in Los Angeles.

Trying Times at Spring Training

Their honeymoon in San Jose, California, was a brief one, so Jackie could report to spring training in Daytona Beach, Florida, on March 1. Rickey told the couple that Rachel had to join Jackie in Daytona. She would be the only wife of a player allowed to come along. On February 28, the newly married couple flew from California to Florida. They had two stopovers, first in New Orleans and then in Pensacola, Florida. Rachel was nervous about facing Jim Crow laws in the South. At the New Orleans

Rachel Robinson: Quiet Strength

Rachel Robinson was born Rachel Annetta Isum in Los Angeles on July 19, 1922. She attended UCLA, and in 1945, upon completing training as a nurse, became the winner of the Florence Nightingale Award for clinical excellence.

Rachel supported Jackie throughout their life together, including his early days with the Dodgers, and worked with him on various civil rights projects. She was calm, poised, and organized, the perfect complement to Jackie's fiery energy. During Jackie's season with the Montreal Royals, a writer for a prominent black newspaper, the *Afro-American*, watched her sit quietly at one of Jackie's games in Baltimore as constant racial abuse swirled around her in the stands. Wrote the reporter: "The only person I know who can equal her is that first citizen of the world, Mrs. Eleanor Roosevelt [the wife of the late President Franklin D. Roosevelt]."

airport, she experienced for the first time the South's deeply rooted discrimination against African-Americans. She defiantly used the "white" washroom, and nothing happened. But then they were told they couldn't board their connecting flight. They waited at the airport for hours before finally giving up for the night and checking into a hotel.

In the morning, they were finally able to fly out of New Orleans, but when they landed in Pensacola they were asked to get off the plane. They were told the plane needed to lighten its load, but it was really a matter of white passengers taking precedence over the Robinsons. At the ticket counter, Jackie almost lost his temper. "I could see him seething," Rachel said. "I thought he might hit somebody in his rage and then where we would we be?"

They went into town, where Jackie decided they would travel to Daytona by bus. He called the Dodgers organization to explain the

situation and tell them he would be late. They boarded the bus. It was humiliating. Once again, Jim Crow reared its head, and they were forced to sit at the back of the bus, where the seats didn't recline. Rachel cried all through the night while Jackie tried to sleep. They finally reached their destination that afternoon. "I had never been so tired, hungry, miserable, upset in my life as when we finally reached Daytona Beach," Rachel recalled.

Waiting for them at the station were Wendell Smith and Billy Rowe from the *Pittsburgh Courier*. Rickey had hired the two writers from the *Courier* to help the Robinsons in any way and to document Jackie's breakthrough into organized baseball. But before he had even started, Jackie was nearly done. He looked at the reporters grimly. "I never want another trip like that one."

After a night in Daytona, Jackie and Rachel moved to nearby Sanford, where the Dodgers were setting up their training camp. They were put up in the home of a black couple because African-Americans weren't allowed to stay in any of the local hotels. The couple made them feel at home, and, feeling rested, Jackie showed up at camp on Monday, March 4. Several eager reporters met him as he walked onto the field for the first time, wearing his Montreal Royals uniform. Asked what he'd do if one of the white pitchers threw at his head, he quickly replied, "I'd duck!" Everyone laughed.

Over the next few days, Jackie played hard and played well, and in many ways proved himself to his future teammates. But prejudice was everywhere. Clay Hopper, the Montreal

Royals' new manager, was from Mississippi, one of the first states to sanction Jim Crow laws. When Rickey, watching Jackie play, said the black player had just executed a superhuman move, Hopper replied, "Mr. Rickey, do you really think a nigger's a human being?" As Jackie wrote later, Rickey was infuriated but restrained himself, explaining to Jackie:

"I saw the Mississippi-born man was sincere, that he meant what he said; that his attitude of regarding the Negro as a subhuman was part of his heritage; that here was a man who had practically nursed race prejudice at his mother's breast. So I decided to ignore the question."

By this time, Jackie Robinson was one of the most famous athletes in the world. Plenty of the attention he received was negative. He took criticism from some supporters of the Negro Leagues, who felt that his entry into the minors might lead to the end of black baseball. There were also, of course, many whites who took offense at Jackie's presence simply because they could not fathom the idea of blacks and whites competing on the same field of play.

Throughout it all, Rickey kept up the positive reinforcement, both for Jackie personally and to the world at large. "If an elephant could play center field better than any man I have," he told reporters, "I would play the elephant." The team started to solidify over the coming weeks, but the extent of what they were up against quickly became clear. The Royals were scheduled to play an exhibition game

WENDELL SMITH: AN EARLY ALLY

Wendell Smith was born on March 23, 1914, in Detroit, where he also grew up. He studied journalism and played baseball at West Virginia State College. No stranger to baseball's infamous color line, he was a skilled pitcher who was once told by a scout, "I wish I could sign you, but I can't." While at school, he became sports editor for the college newspaper. After graduating, he got a job as a sportswriter, then sports editor, for the *Pittsburgh Courier*, a popular African-American newspaper that was read across the country.

An outspoken opponent of segregation in sports, Smith was credited with suggesting to Branch Rickey that he sign Jackie Robinson. Once Jackie was with the Dodger organization, Rickey paid Smith $50 a week to travel with Jackie on the road and write about his experiences. At games, he wasn't allowed to work from the press box with white reporters, so he sat in the stands with a typewriter on his knees. He also worked with Jackie to produce a weekly newspaper column and, later, Jackie's autobiography. In cities that were still segregated, such as St. Louis and Cincinnati, where Jackie wasn't allowed to stay in the same hotels as his teammates, Smith found housing for both of them.

"Smitty" died in 1972, just one month after Jackie. In 1994, 22 years after his death, the man who had brought Jackie's story to life was inducted into the writers' wing of the Baseball Hall of Fame. Even with this belated honor, Smith's contribution to the Jackie Robinson story has been mostly overshadowed by the accomplishments of Jackie himself. Smith's legacy received an unexpected boost, however, in the 2013 Jackie Robinson movie *42*. The voice of Smith's character is the first one heard in the biopic, and his relationship with Jackie and Rickey plays an important role in the story of Jackie's life.

against the Jersey City Giants in Jacksonville. Before the game, the city of Jacksonville sent a notice to the Royals that read, "Negroes and whites cannot compete against each other on a city-owned playground." Hopper and Rickey canceled the game.

Several other Florida towns followed Jacksonville's lead, and the Royals were forced to cancel more games. In one game, the local

Jackie Robinson (last on right) sits with teammates from the Montreal Royals during spring training, 1946. Sitting next to him is another black ballplayer named Johnny Wright. Wright also played in the Negro Leagues and had signed with the Dodger organization around the same time as Jackie. His signing created a lot less fanfare and was probably mostly intended to provide a companion to Jackie during his stint with Montreal. He only lasted a few weeks with the Royals before being sent to a team farther down in the minors. Eventually, he wound up back in the Negro Leagues.

police chief stopped the contest at the beginning of the third inning and told Hopper he had to remove Jackie from the game. Despite these setbacks, Rickey and the Dodger organization pushed ahead with the plan.

On April 18, as a member of the Montreal Royals, Jackie Robinson made history when he took the field in Jersey City in the first regularly scheduled game of the International League season.

A Royal Season

After Jackie's successful debut in Jersey City, he set his mind to the season ahead. The season would be a long one—154 games, not counting any post-season play. Jackie also now had to face, day in and day out, the reality of being the only black player in organized baseball.

Roosevelt Stadium, the home of the International League's Jersey City Giants, was the ballpark in which Jackie Robinson made his debut as a professional baseball player with the Montreal Royals on April 18, 1946.

The team traveled to Baltimore to play the Orioles, which were back then a minor-league franchise. Baltimore had geographic and cultural ties to the U.S. South, and it was as far removed from the Canadian city of Montreal as any other destination in the league. There, white fans hurled insults at Jackie every time he ran onto the field or stepped up to bat.

Rachel, sitting in the stands, heard every word—and it hurt. Jackie gritted his teeth and played ball. "On the good days the cries of approval made me feel ten feet tall, but my mistakes, no matter how small, plunged me into deep depression. I guess black, as well as white, fans recognized this, and that is why they gave me that extra support I needed so badly." The pressure started to cause him health problems. "I couldn't sleep and often I couldn't eat," he wrote later.

Luckily, Jackie and Rachel found a welcoming community in Montreal. They rented a small apartment, and their French-Canadian neighbors were friendly. At the Royals' home ballpark, Jackie found supportive fans. "I owe more to Canadians than they'll ever know," he would later recall. "In my baseball career they were the first to make me feel my natural self." It was just the thing he needed to withstand the abuse he faced on the road. Rachel, too, needed this relief from discrimination. They were still minorities in a mostly white neighborhood, but they made a few friends, and most people they met were kind to them.

In June, settling into this new life, Rachel told her husband she was pregnant. She had known for a few months already, but didn't want to tell Jackie because of all the pressure he faced in baseball. He was thrilled with the news.

Meanwhile, as Jackie's game improved, he slowly started to win over white critics. Even his manager, Clay Hopper, was beginning to see why Rickey had chosen Jackie. In an interview with *Newsweek* magazine, the manager said, "He's a big-league ballplayer, a good team hustler, and a real gentleman." In 1946, the Royals won 100 games. Jackie's hot bat, along with his agility and quick thinking on the base paths and while playing second base, were indisputably keys to this success. He led the league with a .349 batting average and .985 fielding percentage. He also drove in 66 runs and scored a league-leading 113 runs. He stole 40 bases, including heart-stoppers like his theft of home during a game against Baltimore. At the end of the season, he was named the International League's Most Valuable Player.

Post-Season Trials and Triumphs

With the regular season behind them, the Royals advanced through the playoffs and won the International League pennant. Next opponent—the Louisville Colonels, champs of the American Association, in the Little World

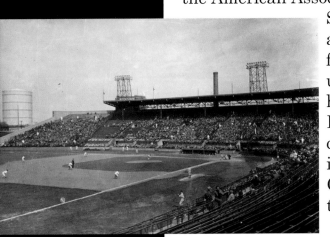

Series. In Louisville, the abuse shouted at Jackie from the stands was almost unbearable, and it affected his performance on the field. Even white newspapers commented on how bad it was. In Kentucky, the Colonels took two out of three games.

When the Series moved to Montreal, local fans were vocal in their support of their team. They also loudly expressed their dislike of the visitors, whose fans had treated Jackie so badly. Back on friendly turf, Jackie got his game back. The Royals tied the Series in Game 4, with Jackie knocking in the winning run in the tenth inning. In Game 5, playing some of the best baseball of his life, Jackie led the Royals to a win and a three-games-to-two lead in the Series.

On October 4, the Royals took Game 6, beating the Colonels 2–0 and winning the Little World Series, four games to two. After the game ended, the fans called Jackie back onto the field. Men and women alike tore at his clothes, kissed him, and lifted him onto their shoulders in triumph. When he finally managed to shower and change, he found a crowd still waiting for him outside the stadium.

Like the city of Montreal itself, Delorimier Stadium, home of the Montreal Royals, provided a friendly, supportive environment for Jackie during the 1946 season. When the Royals ceased operations and relocated to Syracuse, New York, in 1961, the park saw limited use and was eventually torn down.

Baseball Lingo

Since the 1850s, the game of baseball has more or less kept its current rules. Here are just a few of the many terms used in the sport.

- **Balk:** An illegal pitching motion, usually involving pretending to pitch with no intention of doing so. If an umpire calls a balk, any runners on base advance to the next base.
- **Batting average:** A figure based on the number of hits a player gets divided by the number of official times at bat. A highly respected average would be anything near or above .300 (three hundred), which means the player has hit safely 30 percent of the time he or she has been at bat.
- **Bunt:** A method of hitting the ball where the batter holds the bat still and lets the ball hit it, instead of swinging. The point of a bunt is usually to strategically advance players already on base.
- **Double:** A hit resulting in the batter making it safely to second base.
- **Double play:** A play in which two players are out.
- **Error:** A play in which a fielder makes an avoidable mistake.
- **Grand slam:** A home run with the bases loaded, scoring four runs.
- **Inning:** A period in which each team has a turn at bat, until the opposing team gets three outs. Typically, games have nine innings.
- **Lead:** A runner stepping off a base and edging away, to either steal a base or be ready to run if there's a hit.
- **RBI (Run Batted In):** A statistic that credits a batter whose at bat results in a run scored, except in certain cases, such as when a fielder commits an error.
- **Sacrifice:** A play with fewer than two outs in which the batter is out but at least one runner already on base advances to the next base or scores a run from third base.
- **Slide:** When a player slides on the ground toward the base, to try to touch the base before being tagged out.
- **Slump:** A prolonged period during which a player or a team is not doing well.

They cheered and congratulated him, even serenading him with songs. As he ran down the street, headed for the team hotel so he and Rachel could get to the airport, the crowd chased after him. The *Pittsburgh Courier* wrote, "It was probably the only day in history that a black man ran from a white mob with love instead of lynching on its mind."

Moving to the Majors

On November 18, 1946, with Jackie at her side, Rachel gave birth to a healthy baby boy. They named him Jack Roosevelt Robinson Jr. But Jackie didn't have much time to settle into his new life as a father. In February 1947, he was among a few other black players, including a star catcher named Roy Campanella, who went

In 1947, the Dodgers held spring training in Havana, Cuba, in part to avoid the problems the team and Jackie Robinson had faced with racial prejudice the previous year in Florida. In this photo, Jackie, his first baseman's mitt tucked under his arm, signs autographs for fans in Havana as members of the press watch from the dugout.

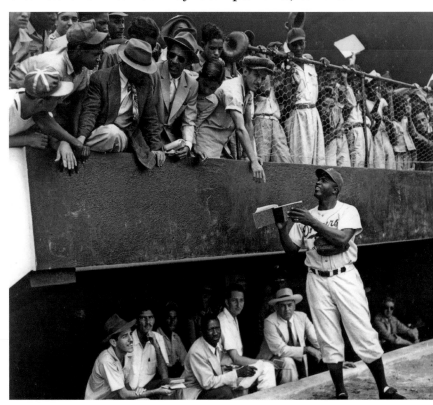

to Havana, Cuba, for the Dodger organization's spring training season. At this point, he was still technically with the Montreal Royals. Jackie didn't know if he was going to move up to play with the Brooklyn Dodgers or not.

A sign came when he was handed a first-baseman's mitt. He'd never played first base before. All the other infield positions were filled, however, so first was the only spot available to Jackie. He steeled himself for the task at hand. The Dodgers and Royals played a series of exhibition games in Cuba, Panama, and finally at Ebbets Field in Brooklyn. Rickey knew what he was doing. "I want you to run wild," he told Jackie, "to steal the pants off them, to be the most conspicuous [visible] player on the field." Jackie did exactly that. He played first base as though he'd been there for years. And he was up to all his usual antics while at bat or on base—bunting, hitting consistently, and stealing bases with his trademark bravery.

The Dodgers' manager, Leo Durocher, was impressed. When interviewed by Wendell Smith of the *Courier*, Durocher was enthusiastic: "He's a swell ballplayer. Jackie can

"This guy didn't just come to play. He come to beat ya."

Leo Durocher

Jackie Robinson and Dodgers manager Leo Durocher shake hands during spring training in Havana. When it became clear that Jackie would be moving up from Montreal to the parent club in Brooklyn, Durocher made some other things clear: Anyone on his team who had a problem playing with Jackie would find himself in Leo's personal doghouse.

hit, run, and field. What more can a manager ask of a player?" Despite Durocher's high praise, not all the Dodger players were as impressed. A petition started to go around the clubhouse, or locker room, to have Jackie dropped from the team. Some of the players even hinted that as long as Jackie was playing, they would not. With Rickey backing him, Durocher put a stop to it. He gathered the team in the middle of the night and shouted at them:

"I don't care if the guy is yellow or black, or has stripes like a ... zebra! I'm the manager of this team and I say he plays.
What's more, I say he can make us all rich.
And if any of you cannot use the money,
I will see that you are all traded."

After Durocher had stopped the petition, it looked as if everything was set for Jackie to be brought up to the parent club. Rickey was busy with his grand plans, but he was suddenly shocked by a scandal that cost him his manager. During spring training, Durocher, whose nickname was "The Lip," got into a public feud with the president of the New York Yankees over charges of allowing gamblers in their respective teams' clubhouses. The upshot of this feud was Durocher's suspension from baseball for the 1947 season for "association with known gamblers."

Now Rickey had two high-profile stories to handle, and he desperately needed a new manager. He was about to break baseball's color line by promoting Jackie Robinson to the Brooklyn Dodgers. And he now had to field questions about what he would do without his manager. But Rickey was made of strong stuff, and he persevered through it all.

On April 10, 1947, members of the press received an announcement signed by Rickey. It read, "The Brooklyn Dodgers today purchased the contract of Jackie Roosevelt Robinson from the Montreal Royals. He will report immediately." Later that same day, Jackie walked into the Dodgers' clubhouse at Ebbets Field for the first time. He didn't have a locker yet, and he had to hang his clothes on a nail. But when he walked into that room, the jersey he was handed had "Dodgers" written on the front, in script. On the back was the number 42.

Au revoir, Montréal, Québec. All aboard for Brooklyn, New York!

Chapter 5
42: A Major Player

In his 1972 autobiography, *I Never Had It Made,* Jackie Robinson wrote, "Whenever I hear my wife read fairy tales to my little boy, I'll listen. I know now that dreams do come true." On April 15, 1947, Jackie lived his dreams when he walked onto Ebbets Field in Brooklyn, wearing number 42 in his first official game in the major leagues. He had already played a few exhibition games with the Dodgers to over-capacity crowds. But this was the big moment. Between his nervousness and the daunting task of hitting the lively curve ball of Boston Braves pitcher Johnny Sain, Jackie's bat was relatively quiet. Although he didn't get any hits, he reached base when he bunted the ball with a runner on first, resulting in a throwing error that allowed him to advance the runner, reach base himself, and eventually score in a 5–3 Dodgers win. It wouldn't take long for Jackie to find his confidence at the plate. In fact, not only his courage and character, but his brilliance as a ballplayer, were about to take the world by storm.

In a scene that would become commonplace over the next decade, Jackie Robinson is photographed walking on the street outside of Ebbets Field, home of the Brooklyn Dodgers, on April 16, 1947, one day after his major league debut.

NG RUN

Jackie Robinson looks to the future.

Jackie Romps Home From Second Base As 26,000 Cheer

By WENDELL SMITH, Courier Sports Editor

EBBETS FIELD, Brooklyn, N. Y.—Here is the p by play account of the Brooklyn-Boston big lea opener as played here Tuesday afternoon before a cr of 26,623.

FIRST INNING

BOSTON— Culler bounded to third baseman Jorgenson, who th to ROBINSON for the putout. Hopp struck out. McCormick sin to center and went to second on a wild pitch. Elliott walked and Litwhiler flied to center.

BROOKLYN—Stanky grounded out, second to first. ROBIN grounded out, third to first. Reiser walked. Walker grounded pitcher to first.

SECOND INNING

BOSTON— Torgeson walked. Masi popped to Reese. Ryan into a fast double play, Stanky to Reese to ROBINSON.

BROOKLYN—Hermanski popped to second. Edwards flied to center. Jorgensen walked and Reese flied to right.

THIRD INNING

BOSTON—ROBINSON made all three putouts. Sain grou out, third to first. Culler was out, short to first. Hopp went ROBINSON.

Rising to the Challenge

In his first week in the majors, Jackie banged out five hits, one of them a home run. He played the unfamiliar position of first base perfectly, recording 33 putouts. Following Leo Durocher's suspension from baseball, Branch Rickey hired Burt Shotton to take over the reins of the team. Shotton, a scout for the Dodgers, was already familiar with most of the talent on his team.

The ballclub was looking good, but morale was still low. While Durocher had made it clear that the players didn't have a choice about Jackie being on the team, many were still unhappy about playing with a black man. Jackie did have a few early allies in players like shortstop Pee Wee Reese, plus the support of Rachel and Rickey, but in many ways, he was alone out there.

That changed when he stepped up to bat against the Philadelphia Phillies on April 22. Led by manager Ben Chapman, members of the Phillies instantly started shouting racial taunts. The insults were of the worst kind, and the barrage was relentless. Harold Parrott, a sportswriter and the Brooklyn Dodgers' traveling secretary at the time, commented later:

"At no time in my life have I heard racial venom and dugout abuse to match the abuse that Ben sprayed on Robinson that night. Chapman mentioned everything from thick lips to the supposed extra-thick Negro skull and the repulsive sores and diseases he said Robinson's teammates would become infected with if they touched the towels or combs he used."

Jackie Robinson and Phillies manager Ben Chapman pose in 1947. This staged photo op was designed to reduce the furor created by Chapman's racial abuse against Jackie. In the movie 42, the story of Jackie's first season in the majors, the "taunting" scene is intense and disturbing.

Jackie nearly cracked. "I tried to just play ball and ignore the insults, but it was really getting to me," he wrote. He said he considered confronting the Phillies and giving up on the whole idea of playing ball. Somehow, however, he kept his cool. In the end, the incident actually worked in favor of the Dodgers. It brought them together. Eddie Stanky, the Dodgers' white second baseman, stuck up for Jackie and yelled back at the Phillies players. "Chapman did more than anybody to unite the Dodgers," Rickey said. "When he poured out that string of unconscionable abuse, he solidified and unified thirty men."

From that game on, the Dodgers seemed to pull together. Jackie, however, fell into a hitting slump. Major league pitchers are tough to hit against at the best of times, and Jackie had the added pressure of being the target of abuse while playing in the national spotlight.

"To hell with Mr. Rickey's noble experiment... To hell with the image of the patient black freak I was supposed to create. I could throw down my bat, stride over to that Phillies dugout...and smash his teeth in with my despised black fist. Then I could walk away from it all."

Jackie Robinson

When, as so often happens to a player in a slump, he did make contact, he often hit the ball directly at a fielder, making him an easy out.

On top of all this, players for the St. Louis Cardinals were planning to go on strike rather than play against Jackie and the Dodgers. The story blew up in the press, and both white and black newspapers lashed out at the Cardinals. National League president Ford Frick threatened the Cardinals with suspension from the National League if they did strike, and the matter ended there.

The Cardinals played the Dodgers in their next series of games, but it would take more than directives from baseball executives to put an end to the bigotry. Jackie and Rickey were receiving a steady stream of hate letters. Some even threatened the lives of Rachel and Jackie Jr. These letters exposed the deep racial hatreds that persisted across the country. While they no doubt made Jackie nervous, he still had Rickey's moral support and, if necessary, police protection.

Meanwhile, on the field, Jackie continued to experience abuse. While dancing off second base against the Chicago Cubs, he was deliberately kicked during a pick-off attempt. When he was fielding, players deliberately slid into him spikes first, tearing gashes into his legs. In a game against the Pittsburgh Pirates, pitcher Fritz Ostermueller threw at Jackie's head. The ball hit Jackie's arm when he tried to block it, and the pain caused him to fall to the ground. Ostermueller's fastball wasn't the only pitch thrown at him. Jackie would be hit nine times that season. Of course, every time he was hit, he was awarded first base. There, Jackie could exact his revenge by taking enormous leads, flustering and distracting the pitchers who had just thrown at him. These incidents tested Jackie's patience, but he kept his promise to Rickey that he would turn the other cheek.

It helped that his support was growing. Now that they recognized his value as a fellow Dodger, more and more members of his team backed him up. Shortstop Pee Wee Reese in particular became a close friend. Jackie recalled a game against the Reds in Cincinnati. Reese had been singled out for abuse as the teammate of an African-American. "They were calling him some very vile names," Jackie said. This abuse, plus the racial slurs directed at Jackie, prompted Reese into action. He walked across the infield and stood next to his black teammate at first base. He quietly put his arm around Jackie's shoulder, and stood there, staring at the Reds' dugout until the hecklers finally fell silent.

"I will never forget it," said Jackie. Rachel later said the moment was incredibly important to her husband. "It came as such a relief to him, that a teammate and the captain of the team would go out of his way in such a public fashion to express friendship." The more he became accepted by his teammates, the better Jackie seemed to play baseball. His hitting slump ended, and he nudged his average up to .283. The Dodgers were closing in on first place.

Jackie Robinson and Pee Wee Reese are featured on the cover of Sports Stars *magazine in 1952. Their pose is a reminder of the moment when Pee Wee walked up to Jackie in the middle of a game and offered his new teammate, and future friend, support in the face of racial abuse from opposing fans.*

Changing Times

Earning the respect and support of his teammates made a huge difference in the quality of Jackie's life with the Dodgers. It did not, however, put an end to the prejudice and discrimination he endured beyond the team's clubhouse in Brooklyn. In other National League (NL) cities, he often had to stay at a different hotel than his white teammates. Often, even when he did stay at the same hotel, he was prevented from joining the team in the hotel restaurant. Incidents like these were not new, but they endlessly gnawed away at his patience whenever the team played on the road.

LARRY DOBY: BREAKING BARRIERS IN THE AMERICAN LEAGUE

Lawrence Eugene Doby was the second African-American baseball player to enter the major leagues and the first to play in the American League. He was also the first black player to go straight from the Negro Leagues to the majors, unlike Jackie, who had a trial year with the Montreal Royals.

On July 5, 1947, the Cleveland Indians bought Doby's contract from the Newark Eagles of the Negro National League, and he made his debut in the American League. He and Jackie spoke on the phone a few times that year, sharing advice with each other. Doby played in the majors until 1960. "Kids are our future," he said, "and we hope baseball has given them some idea of what it is to live together and how we can get along, whether you be black or white."

Meanwhile, on the field of play, the times were changing. In July 1947, the Cleveland Indians made history when they signed Larry Doby, who became the first African-American to play in the American League (AL). In August, Rickey signed Dan Bankhead, who became the first black pitcher in major league baseball. Like Doby, Bankhead went directly from the Negro Leagues to the majors.

With the widely publicized column he wrote with Wendell Smith, Jackie was showing the world that not only could an African-American play good baseball, but he could also be dignified, polite, and intelligent. He once famously said, "I'm not concerned with your liking or disliking me. All I ask is that you respect me as a human being." Alongside most other African Americans, he still faced the harsh reality of prejudice in his daily life. On the playing field, however, Jackie was starting to be seen as an equal—and in some ways, more than equal.

The Dodgers finished the regular season in first place. Jackie led the NL in stolen bases and sacrifice bunts and was second in runs scored. *The Sporting News* named him its first Rookie of the Year, emphasizing that the award had nothing to do with his color:

"The sociological experiment that Robinson represented, the trail-blazing that he did, the barriers that he broke down did not enter into the decision. He was rated and examined solely as a freshman player in the big leagues—on the basis of his hitting, his running, his defensive play, his team value."

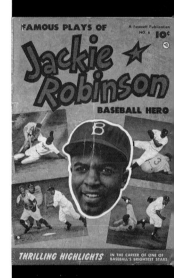

This Jackie Robinson *comic book cover (issue #6, 1951) shows some of the "famous plays" that are featured inside—sliding into third, laying down a bunt, and executing a double play.*

Long-suffering Brooklyn baseball fans waited over 70 years for a world championship, adding fuel to the nickname "Bums" as part of the Dodgers' identity.

The Sporting News wasn't the only publication to recognize Jackie's achievements. *Time* magazine put him on the cover that September, and others ran stories about him on their front pages. On September 23, Brooklyn honored its adopted athlete with Jackie Robinson Day at Ebbets Field. His mother Mallie even flew in for the occasion. At the event, he was given a number of gifts, including a new Cadillac.

A Subway Series and the Noble Experiment

With the regular season behind them, the Dodgers prepared to face a tough opponent from the American League, the crosstown New York Yankees, in the World Series. If Jackie was rattled by squaring off against the mighty Yankees, he didn't let on. "It's a thrill," he told reporters. "I love it." The Dodgers lost the first two games, but won the third and fourth. Jackie's presence was a huge draw at both Ebbets Field and Yankee Stadium, and attendance at both ballparks hit all-time highs.

The Yanks took Game 5, with Jackie knocking in the only run for the Dodgers. Narrowly escaping a loss in Game 6, the Dodgers pushed the Series to the seventh, deciding game. Brooklyn scored first, taking a 2–0 lead in the second inning, but it was all Yankees for the rest of the game. The Yanks took the game, 5–2, and with it, the World Series, four games to three. It was a Series that few would forget.

It was disappointing for Jackie and his teammates to lose that day, but Jackie's debut in the major leagues was undeniably a major success. In the Most Valuable Player (MVP) voting, he came in fifth. "Jackie Robinson" was now a name known across the country. The black athlete from Cairo, Georgia, had broken baseball's color line and held his own against threats, abuse, and discrimination. He had won the respect of his teammates and other players in the league, and captured the attention of black and white Americans alike.

The critical first season was history. Jackie's place in major league baseball was secure. The long history of segregation in the sport was over, and other teams were now scouting the Negro Leagues as well. Joining Jackie on the Dodgers for the 1948 season were two other black players, catcher Roy Campanella and pitcher Dan Bankhead. It seemed that Branch Rickey had pulled off what would come to be called his "noble experiment."

MVP Jackie

Although 1948 would not approach the level of intensity and pressure of 1947, the season had its share of roller-coaster ups and downs for both Jackie and the Dodgers. During the off-season, Jackie went on speaking tours and underwent surgery on his ankle. He started the year out of shape and took some flak for his weight. Leo Durocher was back as manager at the beginning of the season but was later replaced by Burt Shotton. With Eddie Stanky traded, Jackie started the season at his more

"He knew he had to do well. He knew that the future of blacks in baseball depended on it. The pressure was enormous, overwhelming, and unbearable at times. I don't know how he held up."

Teammate Duke Snider

natural position, second base. It was clear from the start of spring training that less attention would be paid to the color of his skin, and more to how well he played the game. Facing criticism about his condition from Rickey, Durocher, the press, and even his fellow Dodgers, he worked hard to get himself back into shape.

Jackie's individual statistics for 1948 were commendable, but not head and shoulders above what he'd done in his rookie season. He batted .296, one point down from the .297 he'd hit the year before. He hit the same number of home runs, 12. He increased his RBIs from 48 to 85, but the Dodgers as a team had a disappointing year, finishing third.

In 1949, both the team and Jackie showed their stuff. Jackie led the National League with a .342 average, 124 RBIs, and 37 stolen bases. These and other stellar statistics helped him earn the National League MVP award.

All eyes are on the play at third as Jackie Robinson slides in safely with a triple in a game against the Chicago Cubs. Jackie's aggressiveness on the base paths became one of his trademarks, particularly in his MVP-winning season, 1949.

Baseball fans voted him as the NL's starting second baseman in the All-Star Game, which was played at Ebbets Field that year. It was the first All-Star Game to include a black player on either squad. Jackie was joined on the NL team by fellow Dodgers Roy Campanella and pitcher Don Newcombe, and Cleveland's Larry Doby played on the AL side. Meanwhile, the Dodgers had an exciting year as a team. They narrowly beat out St. Louis for the NL pennant before falling to the Yankees in the World Series, four games to one.

Now that he was an established, respected player, Jackie finally had the go-ahead to stand up for himself on the baseball diamond. In his first year in the majors, he had quietly

The 1949 All-Star Game marked another historic first in major league baseball—the first appearance of a black player on either side. All three National League stars were Dodgers—Roy Campanella (left), Don Newcombe (second from right), and Jackie Robinson. Joining them was Cleveland's Larry Doby (second from left), the first African-American to play in the American League.

accepted the abuse hurled at him from players and fans alike. Now, as "just another" player, and one of the game's superstars at that, rather than a *black* player with the eyes of the world watching his every move, Jackie started to stand up for himself. He could unleash his irritation. He never went as far as physical violence, but he finally felt he could fight back with words. He stopped backing down from confrontations with other players.

Like most other players, he disputed what he saw as bad calls, arguing with umpires as the situation may have deserved, but stopping short of actually pushing or hitting anyone. "It kills me to lose," he said, when asked about his temper. "I can't stand losing. That's the way I am about winning, all I ever wanted to do was finish first."

Speaking Out

Jackie also came to be seen as a spokesperson for African-Americans on and off the field. As the pioneering African-American ballplayer in a sport still largely dominated by whites, and a person who was known for expressing his views forcefully, he became a person of influence and importance. The National Association for the Advancement of Colored People (NAACP) honored him with its Annual Merit Award in 1947. The NAACP called him "the first man in the history of our country to grip the handle of a baseball bat and knock prejudice clear out of a Big League park." As he continued to play baseball and learned to cope with his newfound fame, Jackie found himself in a position where he could tell the world what he thought about racial inequality.

World-famous actor, activist, and baritone Paul Robeson leads workers in a rousing rendition of the National Anthem at a shipyard in California during World War II. Robeson, who worked on ships in World War I, appeared during the workers' lunch hour to boost their spirits, and the war effort, in the fight against Nazi Germany. It was widely supposed that the House Un-American Activities Committee (HUAC) called upon Jackie Robinson to testify in an effort to cast a shadow on Robeson's patriotism.

In July 1949, he was called to testify before the House Un-American Activities Committee (HUAC) in Washington, D.C. HUAC was a committee of the U.S. House of Representatives that investigated supposedly "un-American" activities of private citizens, government employees, and organizations suspected of having Communist ties. Because the committee could force citizens to testify, those who refused to do so could find themselves on a HUAC "blacklist." Being publically blacklisted, along with other kinds of negative publicity that resulted from HUAC hearings, could spell disaster for an individual or business.

It was widely speculated that HUAC wanted Jackie to disagree with remarks made by African-American singer, actor, and activist Paul Robeson. Robeson had been reported as saying that black Americans would be

"Every single Negro who is worth his salt is going to resent any kind of slurs and discrimination because of his race, and he's going to use every bit of intelligence, such as he has, to stop it."

Jackie Robinson, before the House Un-American Activities Committee

reluctant to fight for a country that had so oppressed them. It was a tricky situation for Jackie. "I couldn't understand why they wanted me," he said. The fact was, however, that Jackie was now popular and well known. His voice, whatever he decided to say, would be heard by millions of Americans, both white and black. Rachel urged him to trust his instincts.

On July 18, Jackie appeared before the committee in what had become a major media event, and delivered a statement. In it, he talked about patriotism and made it

The Life and Times of Jackie Robinson: The Civil Rights Movement

The 1950s and 1960s, the decades most commonly associated with the modern-day civil rights movement, were years of radical change as people worked to get the U.S. Congress to pass laws that guaranteed equal rights for all Americans. They did this through political-pressure campaigns, drives to register African-American voters, massive rallies and marches, and other actions, such as boycotts and "sit-ins" in which people occupied lunch counters and other segregated places as a form of protest. Eloquent and inspirational black leaders such as Dr. Martin Luther King Jr. urged followers to fight in non-violent ways for racial equality and human respect.

The modern-day civil rights movement finally succeeded in pushing politicians to pass laws protecting people against discrimination on the basis of race, religion, and other factors. These laws, collectively referred to as Civil Rights Acts, were passed by Congress throughout the late 1950s and into the 1960s. It is of course impossible to legislate, or declare by law, good will among people in their hearts and minds. Still, these laws have led to changes—in education, living conditions, and the workplace—that have brought people together and, no doubt, helped create positive attitudes and perceptions in ways that we all take for granted today.

clear that he thought black Americans were still Americans, the same as anyone else. He referred to his time as an officer in the Army and only lightly addressed Robeson's remarks. Mostly, he took the opportunity to speak out against racial discrimination.

The resulting media coverage was mostly, but not entirely, positive. Jackie's patriotism was celebrated in the newspapers. Many also felt that he had turned against Robeson by describing as "silly" Robeson's claims about African-Americans not fighting for their country. In any event, Jackie was playing an increasingly public role as an African-American who would help pave the way for the struggles of the national civil rights movement in the 1950s and 1960s.

This prominent role came about partly because of Jackie's popularity. He was charming and charismatic. He looked good in photos and sounded good on the radio. He even starred in a movie about his own life!

But hostility from the public wasn't over yet. In May 1950, FBI agents told Jackie he had received death threats

In early 1950, Jackie Robinson starred in a film about his life called The Jackie Robinson Story. *The movie followed the story of his life and his rise to fame in baseball. This publicity shot shows Jackie arm-in-arm with some of the stars of the film, including Ruby Dee, who played his wife, Rachel.*

in connection with an upcoming game in Cincinnati. "Robinson, we are going to kill you if you attempt to enter a ball game at Crosley Field," read one of the notes. Not playing was out of the question, as far as Jackie was concerned. Pee Wee Reese responded to the threats, joking that all the Dodgers should wear the number 42: "Then they will have a shooting gallery." Jackie played the game without incident, and even managed to hit a home run. Brooklyn won the game.

Slowing Down

As his baseball career wore on, Jackie was, of course, getting older. He had begun his playing days in the major leagues at 28, already fairly "old" for an athlete entering a rookie year in professional sports. By 1955, at the age of 36, the effects of age and the wear and tear of the game had begun to show. He had gray hairs, he was slower, and he had a variety of health issues that repeatedly forced him onto the bench. He also had three children. Jackie Jr. was eight years old. In 1950, Rachel gave birth to a daughter, Sharon, and in 1952, to their second son, David. The strain that baseball put on Jackie's family life, and that family put on his baseball life, was starting to show.

In 1955, Jackie began struggling at the plate (his batting average for that season dipped from .311 in 1954 to .256, the lowest of his career), and he stole only 12 bases. He suffered from old injuries, and he was slower and sloppier in the field. Despite his declining physical abilities, he helped the Dodgers clinch the pennant by September 8, earlier in the season than any

team in NL history. As they had in 1947, 1948, 1952, and 1953, the Brooklyn Dodgers and the New York Yankees prepared to square off in the 1955 World Series.

Jackie and Rachel Robinson with their children, David, Sharon, and Jackie Jr., in 1956.

During the regular 1955 season, Jackie had missed 49 games, and manager Walter Alston tried playing him at third base and in the outfield, partly because of Jackie's diminishing ability at second. As the World Series approached, many wondered whether Alston would play Jackie in the Series at all. Despite his reservations, Alston decided to play him. Jackie provided a Series highlight when he stole home in the opening game, but overall, he struggled at the plate. The Series went the full seven games, and Alston sat Jackie out for the final game. The Series was an exciting one, with the Dodgers winning the last two games, both at Yankee Stadium, to win the Series in seven. It was the first time the Dodgers had ever won the World Series, and the only time while the team played in Brooklyn (the team would relocate to Los Angeles following the 1957 season).

In 1956, ten years after his debut with the Montreal Royals, Jackie started another season with the Dodgers. This would prove to be a year that was, on the national level, as important to civil rights as 1946 had been to the world of sports. The Montgomery Bus Boycott, begun in December 1955 when Rosa Parks was arrested for refusing to give up her seat to a white woman on a bus, helped make 1956 a critical year in the civil rights movement. When the U.S. Supreme Court decided at the end of 1956 that laws segregating Alabama buses were unconstitutional, a major blow was struck against Jim Crow laws in the South.

Segregation had ended in baseball, but the nation's heightened tensions over African-American civil rights affected the game as well. Some white fans continued to "blame" Jackie for having brought about changes in sports that helped fuel the movement for social changes across the country. On the field, he still had to endure isolated racial slurs from players and boos from some fans. But apart from a couple of times when he reacted to

When Rosa Parks, shown here sometime around 1955 with Martin Luther King Jr. in the background, refused to give up her seat to a white woman on a bus in Montgomery, Alabama, her act of defiance became both a symbol and a strategy in the civil rights movement.

the abuse, Jackie kept his cool and played ball. That year, his batting average rose slightly, to .275, and the Dodgers once again won the pennant. They faced the Yankees in the World Series again, but this time they lost in seven games. Jackie homered in the first game and struck out to end the seventh game—and with it, the Series. It was to be the final at-bat of his final season in baseball.

After the season, Jackie felt that his baseball career was coming to an end, and that it was time to hang up his jersey and call it quits. Before he announced to the world, and to the Dodgers, his plans to retire, the team traded Jackie to its National League archrivals, the New York Giants. He had, however, told his wife and children of his intentions, his two sons crying at the news. Before the trade with the Giants could be completed, and more than a decade after he had broken the color barrier and ended segregation in baseball, Jackie Robinson made his decision to retire from the game. "The way I figured it," he said, "I was even with baseball and baseball with me. The game had done much for me, and I had done much for it."

Chapter 6
Into the Hall of Fame

When Jackie Robinson retired from baseball, he didn't retire his drive and determination. He was hired as vice president of personnel with the Chock full o'Nuts coffee company and restaurant chain, becoming the first African-American to hold an executive position with a major U.S. corporation. This position, which he held from 1957 to 1964, was but one part of his life after baseball. Jackie joined the NAACP as chairman for the organization's "Fight for Freedom" drive, a tour that promoted equality for African Americans and raised money to support civil rights efforts. A publicity campaign tagged onto the tour included a poster of Jackie in his Dodgers uniform accompanied by the eye-grabbing line "Time to Score for Civil Rights."

Batting for All Americans

The late 1950s and early 1960s were a time of massive protests, boycotts, and

Jackie Robinson in 1950. Throughout his career as a pioneering baseball player, Jackie was outspoken in his support for civil rights. When he retired from baseball in 1957, his fame continued to lend strength to the cause.

other organized efforts to eliminate racial discrimination. As political pressure in favor of integration increased, racial tensions were also heightened, particularly in the South. Dr. Martin Luther King Jr. was preaching nonviolent protest. The Montgomery Bus Boycott (1955–1956), which Dr. King helped organize, was a successful example of how the African-American public could exert influence over unjust laws without violent confrontation. In December 1956, after a lengthy federal court case, the U.S. Supreme Court ordered the city of Montgomery, Alabama, to end segregation on its city buses.

U.S. troops escort African-American students to school in September 1957. The integrating of previously all-white Little Rock Central High School, in defiance of the Arkansas governor's insistence on enforcing segregated education, was a key episode in the history of the U.S. civil rights movement.

This success led to similar protests across the South, but it also provoked violence from whites. Two days after the Montgomery decision, someone attacked Dr. King's house with a shotgun. (His home had also been bombed earlier in the year, when the boycott was in progress. No one was injured in either attack.) A few days later, hidden gunmen fired on city buses, injuring passengers. And in January 1957, whites angered by the Supreme Court's decision bombed four black churches in Montgomery. It was a time when standing up for minority rights meant putting one's life on the line.

Jackie didn't shy away from this challenge. He used his public profile to promote the issues he had always believed in. "A life is not important except in the impact it has on other lives," he said. "The right of every American to first-class citizenship is the most important issue of our time." Jackie had already inspired millions with his career in major league baseball, but now he felt he could use that sporting legacy to create positive change. He wrote passionate letters to people of influence, including U.S. presidents, and attended rallies and protests, often alongside Dr. King.

After participating in the NAACP's Fight for Freedom tour, he continued to work with the organization as a board member. He also started writing a column for the *New York Post*. Published three times a week, his articles often discussed the theme of racial injustice. His intention, he said in his first column, was to be genuine and honest, no matter what the backlash might be:

"Back in the days when integration wasn't fashionable, he underwent the trauma and humiliation and the loneliness which comes with being a pilgrim walking the lonesome byways toward the high road of freedom."

Dr. Martin Luther King Jr.

"For better or worse I've always thought it more important to take an intelligent and forthright stand on worthwhile questions than to worry about what some people might think."

Taking a very public stand in 1958, he joined Dr. King as an honorary leader of the Youth March for Integrated Schools in Washington, D.C. Over 10,000 people marched in protest against segregation. Jackie was at the front of the march, with Rachel and Jackie Jr. walking alongside him. Later, in 1963, he would join Dr. King at another march, the massive March on Washington for Jobs and Freedom, where Dr. King gave his famous "I Have a Dream" speech.

Jackie also volunteered his time to other civil rights organizations, such as the National Conference of Christians and Jews (NCCJ) and the Southern Christian Leadership Conference (SCLC). His willingness not only to speak

Left: Jackie Robinson and his 11-year-old son David are part of a crowd estimated to number between 200,000 and 300,000 people at the March on Washington in 1963.

Right: Dr. Martin Luther King Jr. is shown with fellow civil rights leaders in the 1963 March on Washington.

THE LIFE AND TIMES OF JACKIE ROBINSON: THE BIRMINGHAM CAMPAIGN

The Birmingham campaign of 1963 was a series of protests led by the Southern Christian Leadership Conference (SCLC) to end segregation in public facilities and downtown stores in Birmingham, Alabama. The campaign included student-led boycotts of retail stores to put economic pressure on business owners. It also included public marches and sit-ins in which black demonstrators simply sat down in designated white-only areas and wouldn't leave. Police arrested hundreds of demonstrators, including SCLC president Dr. Martin Luther King Jr. They brutally broke up peaceful protests using fire hoses and police dogs. Photos, reports, and news footage of these confrontations brought the story into the living rooms of Americans and prompted worldwide support for the demonstrators. The conflict went on for about a month until, on May 10, the city finally agreed to the SCLC's demands. After the dust settled, Birmingham slowly started the process that would bring integration to one of the nation's most racially divided cities, starting with the removal of Jim Crow signs in public spaces.

about civil rights issues, but also to physically participate, showed his commitment to the ideals and earned him the respect of leaders like Dr. King.

A Passion for Civil Rights and Justice

Jackie also started to dabble in politics, supporting politicians whose campaigns aligned with his beliefs. This thrust him even further into the public spotlight. Initially, he supported the Republican Party and actively backed Richard Nixon's 1960 presidential campaign against John F. Kennedy. He said he found Nixon charming and personable, but more importantly, the presidential candidate

Jackie Robinson in 1965, at the age of 46, broadcasting baseball on ABC. Years of chronic injuries and other medical conditions had begun taking their toll on Jackie by the time he reached his forties.

had publicly voiced his support for the civil rights movement. Kennedy, on the other hand, according to Jackie, seemed ignorant of African-American issues.

Later, Jackie praised Kennedy for the president's support of civil rights issues. He also became angry with conservative Republicans who opposed the Civil Rights Act of 1964. Jackie's political stances, including his later support for U.S. involvement in the war in Vietnam—and his perceived "flip-flopping" between political parties—did not escape the attention of political commentators and critics. Jackie backed people and groups who supported his own beliefs, regardless of how unpopular those beliefs might be. This often made him a controversial figure. But underlying all of his political actions was his firm belief in the rights of African Americans. "There's not an American in this country free until every one of us is free," he said.

Jackie's energy and passion for civil rights seemed to be limitless. One groundbreaking cause to which he dedicated his time, energy, and resources was the founding of an African-American owned and operated bank in the large, mostly African-American neighborhood of Harlem in New York City. The idea was that black Americans experienced discrimination on many levels, including finance. For many African-Americans, borrowing money to buy a house or start a business was virtually impossible. Jackie believed it was important for all Americans to have not only equal rights but also equal opportunities in their daily lives. Without economic equality, black Americans would forever be stuck with low-paying jobs and shoddy housing. To help level the playing field, he opened the Freedom National Bank in 1964.

Extra Innings

While all this was going on, Jackie's personal life was like a roller coaster. His retirement from baseball meant two things for his family life. First, he could spend more time at home with his kids. The Robinsons now lived close to New York City in Stamford, Connecticut, on a beautiful semi-rural property. It also meant that Rachel could resume her career. She went back to school for a master's degree in psychiatric nursing. When she completed the degree in 1960, she took a job with the Albert Einstein College of Medicine in New York.

Jackie's health, which had begun to suffer toward the end of his playing days, continued to worsen. Around the time of his retirement from baseball, he was diagnosed with diabetes. This meant he had to give himself daily insulin injections and change his diet dramatically. He also developed hypertension, or high blood pressure, which put a strain on his heart. These conditions were less effectively treated by medicine in the 1950s and 1960s than today. Coupled with a variety of sports-related health issues, like arthritic ankles and an injured knee, they were hard on the now-middle-aged activist. Following surgery on his knee in 1963, Jackie appeared older than his 40-something years. His hair had turned completely gray, and he was now using a cane.

Quite possibly putting a further strain on Jackie's health was his relationship with his oldest son, Jackie Jr., who was growing up to

"I've been up on cloud nine for about 48 hours. I hope I never come down!"

Jackie Robinson, on his being voted into the National Baseball Hall of Fame

be a troubled youth. He felt his father's criticism more intensely than his sister and brother. His relationship with his dad was often strained. He struggled in school, and although he showed athletic ability, at some point he simply stopped trying. For years, his parents had struggled to help their son find his path in life. Eventually seeking psychiatric help, they followed the advice of a counselor and sent him to boarding school, hoping the change would help the boy find some structure and discipline. It would prove to be only a temporary solution.

Troubling Times

In 1962, Jackie got a big morale boost. Just five years after his retirement, and in the first year of eligibility, he became the first African-

THE LIFE AND TIMES OF JACKIE ROBINSON: AN AFTERNOON OF JAZZ

In 1963, Jackie and Rachel held a benefit concert they called "Afternoon of Jazz" on their property in Stamford. The goal was to raise bail money for civil rights activists who were jailed at peaceful protests in the South. These activists included Dr. Martin Luther King Jr., who had been jailed during the Birmingham campaign. Around 500 people attended the first concert, and they raised $15,000, which was donated to Dr. King's organization, the Southern Christian Leadership Conference (SCLC).

The Robinsons continued to host the annual concert on their property for years, raising hundreds of thousands of dollars for civil rights causes. After Jackie passed away, Rachel continued the concert series and donated the proceeds to the Jackie Robinson Foundation. Over the years, the concerts have included performances by jazz legends such as Ella Fitzgerald, Dizzy Gillespie, Dave Brubeck, and Sarah Vaughan. Recently revived as "Jazz on the Grass" in Los Angeles, the concert series continues today.

American to be voted into the National Baseball Hall of Fame. In his acceptance speech, he thanked Branch Rickey, who was "like a father" to Jackie, as well as his mother and Rachel for their support over the years. All three were by his side at his induction into the Hall. He also acknowledged Wendell Smith and other sportswriters who had reported on his career and helped him along the way.

This well-deserved recognition didn't ease Jackie's home situation. Boarding school seemed to help Jackie Jr. at first, but the teenager soon began struggling again. He dropped out of high school and at one point gathered all the money he could find and ran away to California with a friend. Jackie's relationship with his eldest son deteriorated even farther. They barely spoke to each other now. In 1964, Jackie Jr. enlisted in the Army. He was just 17 years old. He told his mother he wanted to take advantage of the educational opportunities the Army offered.

After basic training and a brief visit home, in which he seemed more mature and well adjusted, he was sent to fight in Vietnam. Not long after arriving, his platoon was ambushed, and the young soldier, now 19, was wounded. He voluntarily returned to active duty after a short stay in the hospital. Back home, Jackie and Rachel followed their son's experiences through the letters he wrote home. He described horrific scenes of violence and his growing discontent with the war effort. In one letter to his dad, he wrote, "This is the most miserable place in the world. I can't see why we're fighting for it. When you see somebody

get shot you think what a waste this all is." He was skeptical of his country's motives for fighting a war so far away from home.

Jackie Sr. supported his country's involvement in Vietnam. Even though he worked alongside Martin Luther King in the civil rights movement, he spoke out against Dr. King and boxer Muhammad Ali when they opposed the war. Jackie's stand on Vietnam turned out to place him, some critics would say, on the "wrong side of history." The same was said about other conservative views he had held and his willingness to testify in front of HUAC in the 1950s. This seemed especially so when many other Americans, black and white alike, came to question the war that would divide the nation more than any since the Civil War.

Jackie Robinson Jr. (foreground) leaves a courthouse in Stamford, Connecticut, following his arrest on drug charges in March 1968. He is accompanied by his father, mother, and sister, Sharon.

Jackie Jr. was honorably discharged from the Army in 1966 and sent home. When he got back, he struggled to adjust to civilian life. The war had changed him. For two years following his leaving the Army, he barely saw his parents. In 1968, to their dismay, he was arrested on drug charges. At his court hearing, attended by his parents, he admitted to illegal drug use. Jackie Sr. and Rachel were devastated. Jackie Jr. avoided a jail sentence by agreeing to enter a program at a drug-addiction treatment facility called Daytop Village. The facility was not far from the Robinson home in Connecticut.

That same year, Jackie Sr.'s mother, Mallie, passed away at age 78, and Martin Luther King was assassinated in Memphis, Tennessee. Just three years earlier, in

1965, Branch Rickey had passed away at the age of 84. Jackie was understandably shaken by all of these events. First, he lost the man who was the closest person to a father he'd ever had. Then he lost his mom and a friend and personal hero. "I was plunged into deep contemplation as I thought of the sadness of saying farewell to a man who died still clinging to a dream of integration and peace and nonviolence," he said after attending Dr. King's funeral.

Still Swinging Away

Despite these losses and his declining health, Jackie continued to write and appear at various public-speaking engagements. No longer writing for the *Post*, he now penned a column for the *Amsterdam News*, a New York-based black newspaper. In it, he continued to comment on civil rights issues.

Jackie's doctors told him to slow down. In 1968, likely due to a combination of his heart condition and the intense stress of the events that year, he had a mild heart attack. He was

In the mid 1960s, Jackie remained politically and socially active. Here, he and Rachel are shown with Nelson Rockefeller (standing between Jackie and Rachel), a liberal Republican governor of New York, meeting with a group of African-American newspaper publishers in 1968. Jackie served as Rockefeller's special assistant for community affairs.

also, due to complications from diabetes, starting to lose his eyesight. But Jackie stubbornly kept up with all his projects, including the Freedom National Bank, and even started a new enterprise, the Jackie Robinson Construction Corporation. The company's goal was to build affordable housing for low-income families.

After a few tough years, Jackie Jr. now seemed to be on the road to recovery. He and his father re-established their relationship. Jackie had even started speaking at anti-drug rallies, supporting efforts to help fight the spread of illegal drugs. In 1970, his drug recovery program a success, Jackie Jr. officially graduated from Daytop. Having experienced the program firsthand and shown leadership ability, Jackie Jr. got a job with Daytop as assistant regional director. He started organizing a concert to raise money for Daytop, to be held on his parents' property.

Tragically, on June 17, Jackie Jr. was killed when he lost control of his brother's car while driving home. Ten days later, the family held the concert, partly in his honor. Civil rights leader Jesse Jackson spoke at the event, and recording artists such as singer Roberta Flack and jazz musician Dave Brubeck performed. The concert raised $40,000 for Daytop. For months after, both Jackie and Rachel kept a low profile, deeply saddened and in mourning over the loss of their son.

Stealing Home

In 1972, 25 years after he stepped out of the dugout onto Ebbets Field wearing number 42, Jackie was invited to throw a ceremonial first ball at the World Series in Cincinnati.

Frank Robinson: Baseball's First Black Manager

Born in 1935, Frank Robinson (no relation to Jackie) started his playing career in major league baseball in 1956, Jackie Robinson's final year. He had an outstanding career as a player, winning both the National League and the American League MVP awards and numerous other honors, including NL Rookie of the Year and both All-Star and World Series MVPs. In 1975, the Cleveland Indians obtained Frank Robinson in a trade, named him a player-manager, and made him the first African-American manager in the major leagues. He managed a total of four teams, and he also served as a coach for three teams. His career as a manager or coach extended from 1975–1991 and from 2002–2006. In 1982, he was inducted into baseball's Hall of Fame.

Somewhat poetically, in his first at-bat as player-manager in 1975, he hit a home run.

On October 15, looking frail and supporting himself with a cane, he stood on the field in front of thousands of spectators and millions of TV viewers. He accepted a plaque commemorating his anniversary and thanked the presenters. Then, holding true to his sense of ethical responsibility, Jackie took the opportunity to address at least one battle remaining in the assault on baseball's color barrier:

"I am extremely proud and pleased. I'm going to be tremendously more pleased and more proud when I ... see a black face managing in baseball."

A little more than a week later, on October 24, 1972, Jackie Roosevelt Robinson died of a heart attack at the age of 53. He spoke his final words to Rachel, rushing to her from the bedroom in their home. He held her in his arms and said, "I love you," before collapsing to the floor. At his funeral service, Jesse Jackson delivered a speech to 2,500 people, including Pee Wee Reese, Roy Campanella, and other famous players and teammates from the

RACHEL AND THE JACKIE ROBINSON FOUNDATION

In 1973, one year after Jackie Robinson's death, Rachel founded the Jackie Robinson Foundation to continue her husband's legacy. The Foundation, still operating today, provides scholarships to minority students who come from low-income families. Over 1,400 students have received a total of more than $14 million in scholarships from the Foundation.

Over the years, Rachel has won several honors for her and Jackie's accomplishments. In 2007, she became the only woman, and the only non-player, to receive the Commissioner's Historic Achievement Award. This award is presented to a group or individual the Commissioner of Major League Baseball feels has made "a major impact" on baseball. Rachel received the award in honor of her work with the Jackie Robinson Foundation and for her "contribution and sacrifice to the legacy of her husband." In her memoir, Rachel wrote, "I was the support person so often misidentified as the 'little woman behind the great man,' but I was neither little nor behind him. I felt powerful by his side as his partner, essential, challenged, and greatly loved."

Jackie's widow, Rachel, at the premiere of 42, *the movie about Jackie's first year in the majors, on April 9, 2013, in Hollywood.*

Brooklyn days. "When Jackie took the field," Jackson said, "something reminded us of our birthright to be free. In his last dash, Jackie stole home."

Earlier in 1972, the now-Los Angeles Dodgers had already honored Jackie's legacy by retiring the number 42 from their team. On April 15, 1997, the 50th anniversary of his first game in the big leagues, all of major league baseball followed suit. Halfway through a game at Shea Stadium (then home of the New York Mets), baseball commissioner Bud Selig held up Robinson's number 42 Brooklyn jersey and announced, "Number 42, from this day forward, will never again be issued by a major league club. Number 42 belongs to Jackie Robinson for the ages." It was the first time a number had ever been retired across all of major league baseball. Now, every April 15 is Jackie Robinson Day. On that day, every player, manager, coach, and umpire in the National League and the American League honors Jackie's memory and shares his legacy by wearing the same number—42.

April 15 is Jackie Robinson Day. On that day, every player in the major leagues can be number 42.

Chronology

January 31, 1919 Jack "Jackie" Roosevelt Robinson is born to Jerry and Mallie Robinson in Cairo, Georgia.

1920 With Jerry no longer living with the family, Mallie and children move to Pasadena, California.

1936 Brother Mack Robinson wins silver medal in 200-meter dash at Berlin Olympics.

1937 Enrolls at Pasadena Junior College, where he distinguishes himself in a number of sports.

1939 Enrolls at UCLA and earns distinction of being the university's first four-letter athlete; brother Frank is killed in traffic accident.

1940 Wins National Collegiate Athletic Association (NCAA) broad (long) jump title, beating his brother's record.

1941 Meets Rachel Isum, a 17-year-old student at UCLA; months shy of his graduation, decides to leave UCLA; spends time working and playing football in Hawaii and learns of attack on Pearl Harbor by Japan, and start of U.S. involvement in World War II, while sailing back to California in December.

1942–1944 Serves in U.S. Army, earning rank of second lieutenant.

1944 Faces court-martial over racial conflict regarding seating on a bus, but is acquitted of all charges; receives honorable discharge due to ankle injury.

1945 Plays shortstop for Negro Leagues' Kansas City Monarchs; is recruited by Branch Rickey and meets with him in New York; signs contract with Brooklyn Dodgers organization.

1946 Marries Rachel; makes professional baseball debut with Dodgers' top minor league affiliate, the Montreal Royals of the International League, on April 18; son Jackie Jr. is born.

1947 Makes major league debut with National League Brooklyn Dodgers, on April 15; wins Rookie of the Year award; wins National Association for the Advancement of Colored People (NAACP) Annual Merit Award.

1949 Testifies before House Un-American Activities Committee (HUAC) concerning race and comments made by famed actor, activist, and singer Paul Robeson; wins National League Most Valuable Player (MVP) award.

1950 Stars as himself in biographical movie, *The Jackie Robinson Story;* daughter Sharon is born.

1952 Son David is born.

1955 Dodgers beat crosstown American League champs, New York Yankees, for Brooklyn's first-ever World Series championship.

1956 Plays last season; Dodgers make plans to trade him to National League archrival New York Giants; announces retirement from baseball before trade can be completed.

1957 Joins Chock full o'Nuts coffee company as vice-president; chairs NAACP "Fight for Freedom" funding drive; receives honorary Doctor of Laws degree from Harvard University.

1958 Joins Dr. Martin Luther King Jr. at Youth March for Integrated Schools in Washington, D.C.

1960 Campaigns for Republican Richard Nixon's presidential bid against John F. Kennedy; in future years will switch allegiance to Democrats, partly over civil rights issues.

1962 Inducted into the Baseball Hall of Fame.

1963 Hosts "Afternoon of Jazz" benefit concert to raise bail money for jailed civil rights activists; joins Dr. King at March on Washington for Jobs and Freedom.

1964 Opens Freedom National Bank in Harlem, New York.

1965 Branch Rickey passes away.

1966 Joins New York Governor Nelson Rockefeller as advisor and lends support to Rockefeller's unsuccessful bid for the Republican presidential nomination.

1968 Son Jackie Jr. is arrested on drug charges; enters and successfully completes drug rehabilitation program; mother Mallie Robinson dies; Dr. Martin Luther King Jr. is assassinated.

1970 Jackie Jr. is killed in car accident; Jackie forms Jackie Robinson Construction Company.

1972 Publishes autobiography *I Never Had It Made;* Los Angeles (formerly Brooklyn) Dodgers retire number 42; throws ceremonial pitch in World Series.

October 24, 1972: Jackie Robinson dies of a heart attack.

1973 Wife Rachel Robinson founds Jackie Robinson Foundation.

1997 Major League Baseball (MLB) retires number 42 for all National and American League teams, names April 15 Jackie Robinson Day.

2004 Jackie Robinson Day celebrations are held throughout major leagues on April 15, leading to Jackie Robinson Day being celebrated every year, as well as tradition of having all major league players and umpires wearing Jackie's retired uniform number 42 on this day.

2013 *42,* a biopic about Jackie's first year with the Dodgers, is released. Rachel involved in production and promotion of movie.

Glossary

abolish To formally put an end to something

activist A person who believes in a cause, issue, or political system, and takes action to promote that belief

arthritic Causing pain, stiffness, and decreased mobility in one's joints

bigotry Intolerance toward another person who looks or acts differently

blacklist A list made by a government or committee; includes individuals, businesses, and organizations viewed as suspicious or as conducting activities deemed inappropriate. People or organizations put on a blacklist are typically excluded from employment opportunities or are boycotted

boycott A form of protest that involves voluntarily stopping using a service or buying goods from an organization until certain rules or practices are changed

Civil War The conflict between U.S. states, mostly divided geographically into Northern and Southern states, from 1861 to 1865, primarily over the issue of slavery

color line The denying of rights, facilities, or opportunities to one group on the basis of skin color; also called the "color barrier"

Confederacy Another name for the Confederate States of America; the nation, and its government, formed by slave states in the U.S. South

court-martial A trial conducted within the military, using military law as opposed to civil, or civilian, law

discrimination Unfair treatment based on prejudice

draft The mandatory requirement for citizens to enlist in the military, often instituted during wartime to build a larger military

exhibition game A game played before the regular season, primarily as a part of the teams' training

Fourteenth Amendment An addition to the U.S. Constitution that ensures equal rights for all U.S. citizens

Great Depression A period of worldwide economic crisis with severe increase in poverty that lasted roughly from 1929 to 1939

inequality In racial terms, when one race is treated better than another

injustice Unfair treatment or lack of justice in a particular situation

insubordination Disregard for authority or the refusal to follow orders, usually in the military

Major League Baseball (MLB) The highest level of professional baseball in North America. Within the major leagues are two separate leagues— the National League (NL)and the American League (AL)

minor leagues Groupings of professional teams—most of them affiliated with teams in the major leagues—that are made up of players who have less experience than it takes to reach the majors. In baseball, players are assigned to minor league teams to gain experience and work on developing skills in hitting, pitching, and fielding

morale officer An officer who is responsible for organizing activities designed to keep soldiers happy and responding to soldiers' needs

National Association for the Advancement of Colored People (NAACP) A non-profit African-American civil rights organization formed in 1909 to "eliminate racial hatred and racial discrimination"

Nazis Short for National Socialist German Workers Party; led by Adolf Hitler, the party in power in Germany during World War II

Negro Leagues Baseball leagues created for African-Americans when the major leagues were segregated

pennant The championship given to the best team in a baseball league

plantation Land on which crops are grown and harvested by workers who live on the property. In U.S. history, plantations were places that relied heavily on slave labor and, later, sharecropping systems

prejudice A preconceived belief, opinion, or judgment toward a person or group often based on their race or ethnicity

scholarship Money or an equivalent award given to a student to pay for tuition and other expenses, usually based on academic or athletic achievement and financial need

scout In sports, a person who watches and reports on specific players; scouts often recommend new talent for recruitment

scrimmage A game played for practice purposes, often between members of the same team

secede To officially separate from a group, government, or organization

segregation The separation of groups from one another; in racial terms, segregation refers to the separation of races in daily life

strike A refusal to work, usually to get better pay or working conditions

World Series The championship series of Major League Baseball that is held yearly between the winners of the National and American League pennants. The winner of the World Series is the first team to win four games out of a possible seven. Because it takes place in October, it is often known as the "Fall Classic"

Further Information

Books

Denenberg, Barry. *Stealing Home: The Story Of Jackie Robinson*. New York: Scholastic, 1990.

Frommer, Harvey. *Rickey and Robinson: The Men Who Broke Baseball's Color Barrier*. Lanham, MD: Taylor Trade Publishing, 2003.

Prince, April Jones. *Jackie Robinson: He Led the Way*. New York: Penguin Young Readers, 2007.

Rampersad, Arnold. *Jackie Robinson*. New York: Alfred A. Knopf, 1997.

Robinson, Jackie, and Alfred Duckett. *I Never Had It Made: An Autobiography of Jackie Robinson*. New York: Putnam, 1972.

Robinson, Rachel. *Jackie Robinson: An Intimate Portrait*. New York: Abrams, 1996.

Robinson, Sharon. *Promises to Keep: How Jackie Robinson Changed America*. New York: Scholastic, 2004.

Rosenberg, Aaron. *42: The Jackie Robinson Story: The Movie Novel.* New York: Scholastic, 2013.

Tygiel, Jules. *Baseball's Great Experiment: Jackie Robinson and His Legacy* (25th Anniversary Edition). New York: Oxford University Press, 2008.

Video/DVDs

The Jackie Robinson Story (VHS/DVD). United Artists/20th Century Fox, 1950/2005.

42 (DVD). Warner Brothers, 2013.

Letters From Jackie: The Private Thoughts of Jackie Robinson (DVD). A&E Home Video, 2013.

Jackie Robinson: My Story (DVD). Shout! Factory, 2010.

Websites

jackierobinson.org
This site is the online home of the Jackie Robinson Foundation. Formed a year after the athlete's death, the Foundation continues to preserve his legacy today. This site is mainly dedicated to educational programs run by the organization, but it also has lots of great information about Jackie's life, including photos and links to other resources.

jackierobinson.com
This official fan site has plenty of good background information, links to further reading, and great historical photos, including some from Jackie's life before baseball.

mlb.mlb.com/mlb/history/mlb_negro_leagues.jsp
This sub-page of the Major League Baseball website mlb.com is a great place to find more information about the Negro Leagues and the history of black baseball. The site features great photos, video clips, articles, and profiles of famous African-American baseball players.

vimeo.com/5283826
This link takes you to a video compilation of Jackie Robinson game footage, set to the Buddy Johnson tune "Did You See Jackie Robinson Hit That Ball?"

youtube.com/watch?v=HaT-9l00050
Jackie talks baseball on *The Ed Sullivan Show*.

youtube.com/watch?v=01qMbIOA0pk
A short documentary about Jackie's legacy.

cbc.ca/player/Sports/Digital+Archives/Baseball/ID/1668389956/
A Canadian Broadcasting Corporation (CBC) interview with Jackie about life, baseball, his time in Montreal, and race relations.

Index

About the Author

Matt J. Simmons is a writer based in northern British Columbia, Canada. He loves exploring big mountains and big ideas, the first with his bike or boots and the second with pen and notebook.